UNLOCKING ADMISSIONS
TO TOP COLLEGES
IN US, UK AND CANADA

Get insider tips from students and alumni of Yale, Brown, Cambridge, and More!

NEEL SARAF

INDIA • SINGAPORE • MALAYSIA

"To my Dad, Pankaj Saraf, and my Mom, Isha Saraf: Thank you for your unwavering and unconditional support in everything I do."

CONTENTS

SOME HELPFUL RESOURCES 149

MY CHECKLIST 157

FOREWORD

Being a High School Counsellor myself with over 17+ years of experience, my first thought before reading the manuscript was, will Neel's book have the depth and impact that a similar book written by experienced Counsellors would have?

I was pleasantly surprised, read it from cover to cover (in one go!), and made my own notes as the book gives some great insights into college admissions across the globe. I am very proud of Neel who has put together the perspectives of different students who are presently at different Universities.

Neel has given a good structure to the book wherein he asked the alumni a set of questions on their high school and college application journey. The questions are well thought out and were well answered. *I particularly liked the answer given by Sarvesh Rajkumar (Brown University, Class of 2025) - 'Not every project has to be a large-scale, monumental project: a consistent and meaningful impact on the lives of even 20 people is invaluable'.*

"I urge every parent and student who is embarking on their high and college application journey to read

the book and benefit from the 'pearls of wisdom' shared by the alumni.

— Priya Gupta, Head College
Counselling & Higher Education Program,
The International School Bangalore (TISB)"

INTRODUCTION

"How do I get into my dream college? Where do I even begin?" These were questions that would recur in my mind every time I thought about college. Of course, I'm not alone in this. My peers have been trying to find answers to these, too. The only way that most of them would get clarity on these was through expensive private college counsellors. But I thought that there had to be an easier way to get information on extracurricular choices, good-quality college essays, community service projects and more, without having to pay a mountain of money.

So, I decided to start reaching out directly to students in top colleges in the US, UK, and Canada. I interviewed them and decided to start a YouTube Channel (called 'Graduate Journey') where I could share these conversations with other aspiring students. I figured the best way to get into my dream college was to ask students who successfully got into those colleges about their journey. This helped me get better insights into the entire profile-building process.

This book is, therefore, a collection of a dozen interviews with students from Yale, Brown, Cambridge, Pratt, UIUC, Waterloo and Imperial College London, among others. Their majors range from subjects in STEM to those in Humanities, Business and Finance. Additionally, the book contains a bonus section where you'll get a sense of how you could approach your Common App essay, with some tips from these students and university websites. Lastly, I've created a list of exciting courses that will act as valuable tools for you as you move along your journey. They will help in improving your skills and building your portfolio for your application.

I hope you find the book useful. I hope it gives you the direction you were looking for to tackle that monumental question that we've all asked before, "So, how do I get into my dream college?"

— NEEL SARAF

CONVERSATIONS WITH UNIVERSITY STUDENTS

This section contains conversations with college students who have made diverse choices ranging from STEM, Arts and Humanities, to Entrepreneurial fields. The students speak about their experiences dealing with the application process. They give us insights on how they were able to get into their dream colleges and share how they worked towards building subject-oriented/field-oriented profiles that strengthened their applications.

Furthermore, students compare the requirements of the US universities to those in the UK and Canada. These comparisons offer insightful information about the similarities and differences between the various educational systems of these countries and their priorities while selecting the right candidates.

You will meet the following people in this book:

Ronit Gupta is a student at **Yale University** studying **Economics and Computer Science**. Along with discussing his experiences participating in internships and other extracurricular activities, he also offered some advice on how to write a strong college application essay. For example, to make the essay unique and memorable, he advised concentrating on specific anecdotes rather than generalisations. He emphasised the importance of displaying leadership skills and tangible accomplishments, such as growing a club from a small to a large membership or increasing revenues for a business.

Sarvesh Rajkumar is a junior studying **Biochemistry and Molecular Biology** at **Brown University**. As a perfect scorer (45/45), he demystifies the challenges of the IB and shares his secrets to crafting a standout college application. He delves into unique extracurriculars like an impactful research programme that combated heavy metal pollution. He also recounts how he navigated uncertainties in the application process, offering invaluable advice on the importance of authenticity in applications. One of the things I enjoyed listening to during our conversation was how his time at Brown University exceeded his expectations from it.

Hugh, a graduate of the **University of Cambridge** in the UK, majored in **Natural Sciences** and focused on **Physics**. When we spoke, he shared how this major exposed him to subjects that he would not have normally studied as a physics major, such as Earth Sciences. He explained the admission process of the University of Cambridge, a unique one from those at other UK universities. As a final piece of advice, Hugh shared tips on how students could ace the interview stage, how they could write an impressive personal statement, and what are some methods through which they could manage time and increase their productivity.

Harshita Singh Pahwa, a student at the **University of Waterloo**, had interesting things to say when I asked her about her experience at a Canadian university, a country that many of us have considered applying to. Having applied to four of the most popular countries - the UK, the US, Hong Kong, and Canada - she decided to choose the University of Waterloo due to its co-op programme. She speaks about studying **Mathematical Finance and Statistics** and the possibility of using technology and finance to build her career in quantitative finance. She also enlightened us about the university admission experience as a CBSE student and the different aspects that set Canadian universities apart from those of other countries.

Mehak Kapoor is a junior at the **University of Southern California (USC)** who majors in **Business Administration**. She completed the GCSE and IB curriculums. The fact that she took 4 HL subjects rather than the typical 3 HL subjects made her application stand out. By doing so, she was able to establish her academic rigour and gain an advantage over her peers (i.e., through more college credits) when she started college. Mehak also co-founded a social venture which focused on educating rural girls in Uganda about feminine hygiene. She tells us how she went about it and shares her experience at some of the internships she took up during high school, all of which contributed significantly to her profile.

Jay Rameshwar is a final-year student of **Biomedical Engineering** at the **Imperial College of London**. A lovely tour by the faculty members, a robust curriculum of the course he was interested in, and the city of London were key factors that helped him decide on the university and course that he wanted to pursue. In our conversation, he talks about the process of getting into universities in the UK and the difference between applying to the US and UK universities.

Naaz Khan, a student at the **Pratt Institute** in New York, discussed what her major in **Industrial Design** entails. She also shared how her high school experience helped her land a spot at one of the most esteemed design schools. One of her learnings was to start early enough to find a balance between time spent working on the art portfolio, the IB core components, and the extracurricular activities. She spoke in detail about putting together a strong portfolio and what colleges look for. She cited some examples of how different universities had different requirements vis-a-vis a student's portfolio.

Vihaan Shah is a first-year student at **Emory University**, who is leaning towards a **Business Administration** major and is at the same time interested in **QSS (Quantitative Science).** He helped organise the first Math Olympiad at Hill Spring International School and has participated in many of them since then. In our conversation, he talks about how students could go about getting good recommendation letters and who the best people were to get these from. He also explains the importance of getting Common App essays ready before the 12th grade and finding value in extracurricular activities even beyond the college application process.

Leah Divecha is a sophomore at the **University of British Columbia (UBC)** student. Although she plans to pursue a **psychology** degree, Leah's robust portfolio, thanks to her training in music, helped her get admission into one of Canada's leading universities.

Kush Gupta is a recent graduate from the **University of Illinois, Urbana-Champaign.** He majored in **Computer Science and Mathematics.** Every year since the ninth grade, he would spend his summer working as an intern at Dell. This helped him get a clear understanding of the workings of major tech companies. Today, he is building his career around data science. During our conversation, he generously recommended a variety of online Computer Science courses that he had found helpful while he was in high school and university.

Nandini Narkar is a freshman at the **University of Arts London** who is majoring in **Critical Practices in Fashion**. From photography to journalism, her fashion portfolio had it all. During the conversation, she advised prospective applicants on how they could create a fashion portfolio (when to start, what to include, etc.), approach the statement of purpose (UCAS), and integrate IBDP into an application, among other things. Her high school experience provides a valuable roadmap for those aspiring to pursue fashion in the UK.

Arnav Gandhi is a freshman at the **University of Southern California (USC)** from Abu Dhabi. A budding content creator on Instagram and TikTok, Arnav is majoring in **Economics** and planning to do a **Media-related minor.** From acing A-levels to navigating the SATs and managing his content creation journey, Arnav reflects on the significance of passion-driven extracurriculars which include collaborating with the United Nations (UN), completing internships with globally renowned firms, and more.

Yale University: Ronit Gupta

Year of graduation: 2024

Major: Economics and Computer Science

Other universities that were applied to: East Coast Schools, IVY League, USC, UCLA, and Stanford.

How has your college experience been so far?

I think last year was a little bit difficult with covid because a lot of our classes were online. It was hard to get a feel for the in-person classes and the professors' teaching styles. But now that we've come to an in-person class, it's got a lot better. I've been able to interact a lot more with other people in the classes and the teachers a lot better. I really enjoyed my first semester of sophomore year.

That's really good to know. You say your areas are Economics and Computer Science. I was wondering with this combination of subjects what your future career prospects were like.

I'm currently interested in either somewhere in technology or somewhere in finance. I'm looking at careers in both of them and also at the intersection of both, like a hedge fund or quantitative finance sort of work. With these subjects, the common careers that usually open up include quant-side work for investment banks, private equity firms, venture capital firms, or hedge funds.

Got it. And have you done any of that kind of work or internships?

In the past few years, I've worked at tech companies. I've done software engineering, but I haven't done any finance work specifically. This summer I'll be doing work in Investment Management. I'm trying to get a feel of how that will be.

And what subjects did you take in high school?

I took AP Chemistry, Physics, Math, Computer Science, Microeconomics and Macroeconomics. I also took World and US History, and then, English for all four years. I took two years of Spanish Language and a year of Chinese language.

Would you mind sharing your AP scores with us?

I got fives on all of the AP exams that I took.

Congratulations! Apart from AP, were there any other courses that helped you earn extra credit?

In the Math department, I took multivariable calculus and linear algebra, and in Chemistry, I took Organic Chemistry.

And in Computer science, I took elective courses, such as Data Structures and Computer Vision.

A lot of students take pressure when it comes to adding extracurriculars to their profile. Could you share some of the extracurriculars that you did so that students can get an idea?

Sure. I was the head of a business club at my school. It was a business competition club, similar to Debate or Model UN, and we did it for business case studies. So, we'd go to competitions and we'd participate in business case studies in individual and team competitions.

I was also the head of a start-up at my school that printed custom apparel. We printed apparel for clubs, sports teams, etc. Then we earned revenue and we put that revenue back into the business. I managed the operations, the finance, and the people management of that business.

I was also the head of the Indian and Pakistani cultural club at my school.

Which do you recall as being the key competitions that you took part in or activities that really made you stand out from the rest of the crowd?

I think the ones that I mentioned were pretty important. In terms of the Business Club, I made it to the international competition, so I spent a lot of time on that and developed the club a lot. We started the club with about five to ten members. But by the time I was a senior, we were up to 50 members. So, basically, the growth and leadership I had kind of displayed through that club was really, really valuable.

Also, in the business venture that I mentioned earlier, I was able to raise revenues from a couple of hundred to 500 at the beginning to multiple thousands – three to four thousand dollars a year in revenue – for this apparel. Showing the accomplishments in numbers of how I was able to grow and develop in these clubs was again super important.

Something that I didn't mention earlier was my work experience. During the Summers, I interned at a technology startup based out of Boston. I did stuff from product marketing to technologies to software engineering to business development. I could talk a lot about my experiences there, what I learned, and how I gained experience in technology, which is what I wanted to major in in college.

How did you go about even getting the internship? Because if students don't have the connections, it's quite hard for them to get an internship.

It was the winter of my freshman year and I was looking for an internship for that summer. I live in the Boston area. So I emailed hundreds of Boston startup companies with a very basic resume and a basic LinkedIn profile, and I said, *I'm interested in working for you.* I asked them if they hired high school interns.

I sent hundreds and hundreds of these emails. It's difficult because a lot of companies, even startups, aren't looking to hire high school students. But I sent a lot of them, and out of those hundreds, I got two to three emails back. These led to three interviews, and then one company decided to hire me. So, I worked with them for all three summers of my high school. After I did well the first year, they kind of brought me back for the next year. That was a good way to get a lot of good experience, but ultimately it also just came down to cold emailing a lot of different places and hoping one will work out.

Wow. And how did you go about balancing your time with your internship during summer, and all the extracurricular work that you were doing?

It was difficult in the beginning because I took on a lot of extracurriculars initially. But I got into a kind of a rhythm and I got into a lot of habits. I think the best way to manage your time is to plan out your week ahead of time and make sure you know exactly where you're allocating your time. It's really easy to get overwhelmed with a lot of AP classes and a lot of homework, but if you schedule your time out in a way that makes sense, it can ease the work. Don't overload yourself. Understanding how long you'll be spending on every extracurricular and actually sticking to that goal, devoting that amount of time to it and to every class, and making sure to plan that out ahead of time is important. It's very manageable then to manage your time. As I mentioned before, it's easy to get overwhelmed, but that's only if you don't have a plan. If you have a plan in place everything works much more easily.

Were there any specific tools that you used for this?

Not any tools specifically. I mostly just used planners or note apps, to-do lists, and stuff like that. The reminders app is great, where I could just note down my priorities. Making priority lists is the best way to do it, or at least it was for me.

I think another big thing for students is community service and CAS work. I'd love to know what CAS work you did and how much time you put into it.

The community service I did was through my school. I volunteered at a local elementary school, a K-5 school, and I was a teacher's aide in a classroom, for students in grades ranging from kindergarten to fifth grade. That was about two to three hours a week for most of my high school.

I also worked in an after-school programme. I spent after-school hours working with students in that same kindergarten through 5th grade age range. That was another hour or so per week.

Circling back then in the summers, apart from the internship, did you do anything else – participating in specific competitions or any specific summer schools?

Outside of work, I went to some summer programmes. One of them was at the University of Pennsylvania, Wharton School. They have a business programme called 'Leadership in the Business World', where I did Entrepreneurship, and started building from the ground up. I learned how to create startups while doing the entrepreneurship programme there.

Then, I also did one at Northwestern University called 'Launch X'. Those were the two programmes, both around startups and entrepreneurship. I learned a lot and was able to get hands-on experience starting a company. Working with a team and going from ideation all the way up to a prototype, I learned so much from those programmes.

Did you also start your own company? A lot of students have interesting ideas and that's one thing they're always looking at – starting something themselves. But they also sometimes force themselves to do it just because it seems important.

We started a company to some extent: we got to a prototype and we worked towards creating an LLC (a limited liability company). But after a while all the members of our team had other things going on during the school year, so it kind of fell apart. We didn't exactly get to launch or get to selling products, but I think throughout the journey from starting into ideation all the way through prototyping, we learned from this experience.

I think if you're genuinely interested in something, you have an idea that you want to work towards, it's also really important to have a good team. If you have a team that you want to work with, that's great, but I don't think forcing yourself to start a company is really going to help you.

Got it. And were there awards that you won during your high school years? I believe that's another thing that can really add to a student's school experience, if not work.

Yes, I made it to the international round of that business competition, and I won some smaller awards at school. I also qualified for the American Invitational Math Exam, the AIME. Those were the kinds of awards that I remember most clearly.

Do you have any tips for our students about building their college profile?

The biggest tip I think I would give is to centre your profile around something. Instead of doing five or six random activities, try to find out what you're really interested in, and do a couple of different activities around that. For example, I was interested in technology and entrepreneurship, so my activities revolved around business competitions, starting a company at these entrepreneurship programmes, running a student business club at my school, and stuff like that. That's how a college can see a coherent profile, and they can understand who you are, what your interests are, and how you're going to take that into college.

When I was applying as a Computer Science major, they could see that I'd done Computer Science work in the past at the startup. During the summers, I had also taken computer science classes and I'd also done this entrepreneurship work. I was interested in maybe starting a company in the future, and that matched their resources. Yale has really good resources for entrepreneurship, for example, the Tsai Center for Innovative Thinking (Tsai CITY). They could see, *okay, this kid is a good fit for our Tsai CITY so they could take advantage of our resources really well or of our Makerspace. Oh, it seems like he'll be using that because he's done stuff with that in the past.*

If a college can look at your profile and say that this is where they'll fit in, that's a really big advantage for you because they know who you are as a student and what you're really interested in. And if that aligns with the school and with the resources and they understand that you are the best applicant to take advantage of those resources really uniquely, then that makes you a better candidate than someone who's maybe really good at stuff but is also really good at five or six different random things. What makes you distinctly qualified at each school?

Also, another big part of that is doing your research about the school itself and seeing based on your profile and your interests, what can you actually take advantage of? Why do you want to go to Yale, for example; what do they have that can help with your interest?

All right and if it's not repeating, are there any specific tips for the essay – when to start writing, how many drafts, etc.?

The essay tip I have is that the summer before the application is due, try to make sure your Common App essay is done. When the supplemental essays are released later, you have time to focus on those. If you can get the Common App essay done before that, it relieves a lot of stress later.

In terms of drafts, I would say just keep writing a lot. When you're starting, don't get stuck on one idea, but write five to ten different drafts, and they don't need to be full drafts. Maybe they can be one to two paragraphs each, but just get an idea and write it. Write as much as you can about it, and then move on to the next idea until you have a lot of different drafts. Then, narrow it down from there and keep revising/rewriting because it's easy to get stuck on one idea. But if you just keep writing, you'll more often than not, find things later on that are more interesting than your initial ideas.

For the supplemental essays, my biggest tip is to do research on every school. So if they're asking *Why Yale?*, you go to the website, and see what Yale has that other schools don't have. Why do I exactly want to go to this school? What courses do they offer? What degree programmes are there? Do they offer things that are different from other schools? What kind of buildings or grants or opportunities do they have that another school won't have? Talking specifically about those in such essays makes you stand out. The rule is if you can just copy and paste a *Why X School?* essay into another application and just change the name and say *Why Z School?* then the essay is not strong enough. If it can just be taken as a template and moved, it's too generic. It has to have aspects from that school specifically.

Things to Remember

- Supplemental essays - make sure the essay is not generic. Research about the various resources and facilities that universities in particular you could take advantage of and mention them in the essay. The more in-depth the research the better.

- Plan your entire week ahead of time so that you can allocate enough time to your different extracurriculars and school work as well.

- Don't need connections to get internships. With enough determination, you can cold email numerous companies in your area and secure an internship for the summer.

Brown University: Sarvesh Rajkumar

Year of graduation: 2025

Major: Biochemistry and Molecular Biology

Other Universities Applied To: UChicago, Vanderbilt, Cornell, Princeton, Stanford, MIT.

High School Programme: International Baccalaureate® Diploma Programme (IBDP)

There's so much to find out about one of the most reputed institutions across the world, Brown University. I want to briefly ask, before that, about your experience with IBDP because it's a rigorous and gruelling board.

Well, looking back, the IB was challenging, even in the context of college, especially the subjects you do at HL level. They give you credit or placement credit at least at the college level, so they're very much introductory college-level classes that you're taking. I feel that having a sort of well-rounded curriculum – not just technical information – equips you with solid research skills, which I feel is pretty unique to the IB. That has helped me in college in terms of my assignments. It has helped me develop that sort of intuition. I'd say that was honestly my main takeaway from IB.

There's also the aspect of learning to manage time because college involves a lot of self-motivation. No one's here to push you and force you to do things. TISB (Sarvesh's high school) gives you a fairly good framework within which to work. All our deadlines were pretty early. We had multiple drafts of everything, which at the time seemed a little annoying, but in hindsight, you realise how useful it was. It teaches you to work in a way that ensures good results for you in the future.

Right and can I just ask what your predicted grade was and what your actual grade for the IB was?

TISB predicts out of 44: my predicted grade was a 44 and my final was a 45 but I did give it that year that we didn't have exams so it was mostly just IAs (Internal Assessments) and PGs (Predicted Grades).

I'm sure to get into an Ivy League, you would have had to do a lot of extracurriculars as well alongside IB. How were you able to balance everything out?

It was a little different for us because a majority of our 11th and 12th went in covid. I was at home most of the time, which limited the number of things I could do. But when you're sitting at home and you're bored, then you're also forced to do things. If you make time for it, there are enough extracurriculars to look at and do things outside of your classes during IB.

The way high school works is that the workload tends to be heavier closer to the exams, closer to deadlines. You do have pockets of time when you aren't doing too much outside of attending classes. Make use of that time to come up with ideas and carry out your projects. Have some kind of idea of what are the things that you might want to do through your college, even things that you would want to put in your essays. Application season can be crazy when it comes to your first term of the 12th grade. It can be really hectic, especially writing all these different essays and coming up with your shortlist. Just taking a look at what the prompts are, coming up with ideas in that free time early enough and being in that mind-space really helps. Most of my essay ideas came to me in my shower like this.

Great! Were you also doing AP Courses?

For me, the IB was enough. I was doing all the subjects I liked. At the college level, AP is viewed at the same level as an IB HL subject. I feel the IB is an extremely well-recognized curriculum, so they understand the skills that it gives you, which the other curriculums may not. TOKs and EEs, etc., are all being taken into consideration, so I don't feel you need to give APs. At the same time, it's not going to hurt you if you do. If an admissions officer sees that you've done two or three APs outside of your IB subjects, I don't know how much it adds but it can't hurt.

Yes, that does make sense. What about standardized testing? Since you were in the covid batch, did you still end up taking the SAT and ACT?

I gave the last SAT before covid. I think our school closed on Friday, and then I took the SAT on that Saturday. I did submit my test scores, but there was pretty much an even split in our year of the number of people who submitted test scores versus those who didn't. Is the test-optional policy still there?

I think so, yes.

At this point, they're used to evaluating applicants without the SAT score so the SAT is kind of a hit or miss sometimes. If you do give it and you feel you're not satisfied with your score and you're ok not submitting it, it's alright.

Do you mind me asking you about your score?

I got a 1570, with an 800 in Math and 770 in English.

Congratulations, that's amazing. We've spoken about different aspects that strengthen the application. Of course, extracurriculars can make a difference in the application. Which ones do you think made you stand

out, especially in the eyes of an Ivy League admissions officer?

The top activity of mine was research. I did a research programme in the second term to the summer of after 11th grade. It was in environmental chemistry. I did this through a programme that connects you with a professor here. You get to work on some aspects of the research with them.

It's not directly related to what I study now, but it did give me a lot of research skills. I focused on that part a lot. I feel having the environmental aspect of that helped as well in that it was rigorous research but it did have some sort of beneficial aspect to it. It was meaningful; my project was to do with heavy metal pollution in the Ganga, so it was close to home. I feel like that was a plus for me.

In the activities list, you're supposed to rank a maximum of 10 activities, in the order of how much they mean to you. I feel like people sometimes tend to choose more showy things and put them on top as opposed to putting things that they consistently did for four years. My second and third activities were not fancy. I played the violin — I was in the orchestra — and I played badminton as well pretty consistently. Those two things were active parts of my life, and even though I wasn't some national-level champion, I still wanted to highlight that. I remember I put those as number two and number three on my list. I don't know how much that contributed to my application, but that's something I don't think you should shy away from doing.

Right, that adds a certain element of authenticity in a way.

For sure! The fact that you do anything for four years consecutively and consistently does say something. You should do those things and put those things down there.

Outside of that, I was the social service prefect for my year and I played a decently big role in Vivum (TISB's School Fest). Then, we organized a national music competition. It was online, much like our Vivum, but I was pretty proud of it. We got submissions from all over the country and we had professional musicians judging the competition. It was a good experience but I do feel that covid changed some of my plans a lot. To be completely honest, when I was applying, my extracurriculars were probably the area of my application I was least confident in. I felt like it was something I could have worked on to give it some sort of shape. Luckily it got me in here, but at that moment it was perhaps the thing that I was least secure about.

And the research programme you did... Was that through Lumiere Education?

I did it through Pioneer Academics. Three or four people in my year did it, I remember. I don't know if it's still popular.

Yes, it is still quite well-known. What about social work which is also a requirement sometimes? I know covid did limit a lot of opportunities, but how were you able to showcase that aspect in your application?

I can't believe I forgot to mention this, but I love teaching. It was a big part of my application. It was what I wrote my essay — my main Common App — about. It was there in my activities list as well.

During my summer after 11th grade, I made an English course for factory workers at an industrial place in Tamil Nadu. There were a lot of textile factories. I made an 8–12-week English course to teach spoken English to people, so they would be able to communicate in the language and were able to advance in their jobs. I feel like speaking English is a fairly important skill in India, even more so today. And I always loved to teach. So, this was a natural thing to do for me.

What was the scale of this like? Some students have certain misconceptions that maybe their social project has to help the entire country.

I'm glad you brought that up because that is not the case. I was teaching 20 people. It was not that much. I remember going on YouTube and looking at what people do to get into college. They would be doing several things and getting awards from the government. I would just be a little overwhelmed in some moments because I'd think, why is this something that's expected of a high schooler. You're 17-18, you're supposed to be living life. Those are things you would be able to do better in five years with a college education.

I don't mean to discourage anybody who has really far-reaching, large-scale ideas. But at the same time, I do believe that it's possible to navigate the high school experience without feeling the pressure of having to do something like that. You don't need to do something that's affecting 50,000 people, because the resources you have are limited. The application process also values smaller-scale things that still had a meaningful impact on some people. Don't feel that pressure of having to do something that's necessarily large-scale. I've been through that rabbit hole of watching YouTube videos. I felt that I wasn't doing enough. If you want to put in effort and you have an idea from the ninth grade, go for it, of course. But it's not the end of the world if you don't, that's all I want to say.

Yeah. I'm so glad you spoke about this. We are creating this platform at the Graduate Journey so people can get inspired about what successful students did, but also to not let students get overwhelmed at this stage. So, thank you for saying that. Apart from this, did you do any internships, or was research just taking up most of your time?

The summer after my 10th grade, before I started the IB, I did an internship at a pharmaceutical company. Here, I was mostly shadowing; it wasn't much lab work. I got to see how the whole process works and what the industry is like for the field that I'm interested in. And it's something that I like.

In fact, design and pharmaceuticals are still something I'm looking at. I also went on this Spiti Valley expedition that TISB takes you on every year. You go into the mountains in Himachal Pradesh and then you do some social work and you also hike. So that's what I did for the first part of my summer and then I was doing the internship for a month after.

How did you manage to get this internship?

It was my dad's friend's thing. So it was just connections. I tried to email one company to see if they had an internship opportunity but they never got back to me. And I feel like that's usually how it is. It's hard to find companies in India which have a streamlined process for high school internships. I haven't heard of any, to be honest.

And what did your awards, prizes, competitions and honours essentially look like?

Nothing too big. I did a bunch of MUNs and got some awards there. I think I put that in there. I also had my music certifications for Ireland. The awards and honours section has been designed keeping the American school system in mind, where there are a lot more opportunities to get these awards and honours.

Even when we were applying, our counsellors told us not to focus too much on having awards because that's just not how the system is designed. And I think admissions officers are well acquainted enough with the Indian system to know that. If people were ranked the IGCSE World Topper, etc., then they would put that there. But it isn't as streamlined of a process as it is here, so don't put too much pressure on yourself for that.

Were TISB counsellors enough for the whole application process? How did you navigate through it?

Yes, I didn't have an external counsellor; I just used TISB resources. I was assigned a counsellor, Ms Priya, who is the head college counsellor, and then we were assigned to another counsellor. I felt like that was enough for me, in terms of the assistance that was required for the application.

I also didn't want to have too many voices weighing in that weren't mine. I wanted a certain amount of control over my application. Going into it, even in the 10th grade, I had decided that I didn't necessarily want external help with my application.

Now, I wouldn't advise directly for or against having an external counsellor because having one did work well for a lot of people. It gives you that fresh perspective and their experience is valuable; one-on-one attention does help. I know a lot of people who benefited from that. But personally, I always knew that I didn't want one, and that worked for me. Ms. Priya was very good; she knows a lot. She gave me the necessary guidance whenever I needed it.

What led you to pick Brown specifically over others? You mentioned Vanderbilt as one of the colleges you applied to as well.

TISB has a short 13-college requirement; we can't apply to more than 13. I chose to apply to Brown over a lot of other colleges because I had heard that the culture here was very down-to-earth. It's very grounded in learning for the sake of learning, and people are genuinely motivated here. It isn't cut-throat, competitive, etc., which a lot of colleges are. That was very much the impression I got before I applied and it has the reputation of being a quirky Ivy college, too.

Has your impression of Brown changed after you've spent a year there?

It's not changed. All of those things that I thought would be true are true, and I love being here. I'm having a great time.

Something that also stood out to me here was the academic flexibility. I feel like colleges in the US give you a lot more of that than colleges elsewhere. I also prefer the US a lot more than other countries because I knew what I wanted to study and I'm still doing that. But at the same time, I'm someone who loves studying other things and needs to study other things. Every semester here I make sure to take a humanities course, regardless of what I'm doing with my major. I feel like having that freedom is something I value.

Brown has something called the open curriculum where you do not have any core requirements outside of your major. You're free to take anything you want. You can structure your education however you want and I feel that having that responsibility was quite exciting for me when I was applying. I spoke about it in my essays as well.

How did you go about getting the best people to write letters of recommendation for you for institutes like Brown?

I think letters of recommendation are possibly, potentially more important than people think they are there. From an admissions officer's point of view, I've heard them say that it's really important. I can see why as well because it gives them an account of you that's entirely not yours, or at least in theory, entirely not yours. That helps them see how you would fit in an academic setting.

In general, hearing really good things about you from somebody else is always a plus. Choose your recommender well. Brown allows you to submit three recommendations, usually it's two or three for others as well. I requested them from my biology teacher, my chemistry teacher, and my history teacher. I was in TISB for a long time. I joined in the fifth grade, and my history teacher in IB taught me every single year from sixth grade. She knew me quite well and has seen me grow up. I was very fortunate to be able to get a recommendation from someone like that. I think that hopefully reflected well on me.

Biology and chemistry, of course, were relevant to my major and what I wanted to study. I did have a good rapport with those teachers as well, even if they taught me for a much shorter period. It can be tricky to build relationships with all teachers, especially if they've taught you for only two years. But even if they say one unique thing about you in their letters, that's enough for it to stand out. The bulk of recommendations are the same: *This person was like this.* One anecdote, however, makes it enough to stand out because those are the margins at this level.

Don't pressurize yourself too much thinking about how you're going to build a good relationship, but focus on being your authentic self. Ask questions to show that you're interested. I'm sure that part will work itself out.

I also had a recommendation from my research professor.

And if you had to go back and give yourself or someone in your position any advice, what would that be?

Brown allows you to submit a video portfolio, something like a video essay. It's two minutes usually and you're free to talk about whatever you want. I think my video showed parts of my personality that are hard to show in writing. It was light-hearted. It just showed me doing things like interacting with my friends, etc. If you have the opportunity to do one of those, do it because it really adds a whole new dimension to your application.

Another thing is that I would be overwhelmed by the fact that one decision is going to affect the next four years of my life. In March, the year when I was in the 12th grade, I had no idea where I was going. In April, I suddenly knew I was coming to Providence, Rhode Island and I would be here for the next four years of my life. Of course, it's a big decision, right? If I had chosen to go to Vanderbilt instead, my life would have been quite different. But as uncertain as this process is, it's designed in a way that you'll always come out of it having gained a lot. Ultimately, yes, maybe it will influence the path that you take in life, but rarely would you go somewhere and absolutely dislike it there.

A lot of it is about making the most of what you have and what you get. MIT was my dream school and Brown was not even in one of my top three. I was aiming high. Brown was my fourth choice in terms of the schools I'd applied to. But I love it here! I can't imagine myself being anywhere else. I'm not gutted that I didn't get into MIT. If you don't get into your dream school, it's fine.

We're incredibly privileged to be able to access this level of education. Even the top 50 schools in this country will give you more or less as many resources as the others. The differences are very, very minute, definitely more minute than we think it is. So, it's not the end of the world if your expected outcomes don't end up happening.

You don't need to be a national hero, do as much as you can do and be as genuine as you can. I feel it will shine through in your applications. 100 per cent of the time, there's more in college (wherever you end up) than you could exhaust your time with; there's always something more to do.

Things to Remember

- Don't be afraid to arrange the activities list in the order that the activities mean to you, instead of placing them in the order of their impressiveness. This helps add authenticity.

- If you have the option, always submit a video portfolio/presentation to add a dimension to your application.

- Not every project has to be a large-scale, monumental project: a consistent and meaningful impact on the lives of even 20 people is invaluable.

University of Cambridge: Hugh

Year of graduation: 2021

Major: Physics (Natural Sciences)

High School Programme: OCR

Can you talk a little bit about the Natural Sciences programme that you're majoring in at the University of Cambridge?

It's kind of like the science lessons at school where you study all the different kinds of sciences. So broadly speaking, that's Biology, Chemistry, and Physics, and then you get to specialise in one of those. I studied Physics. I was actually very keen right from the get-go to study it. It's quite a cool degree because you're almost forced to study a lot of other things as well. For example, in my first year, I studied Earth Sciences, which isn't something you would necessarily do if you're just majoring in Physics, perhaps. It was a great experience.

And when you were applying to the universities, did you apply to the US and the UK or were you looking strictly at the UK?

I actually just applied to the UK. A lot of people from my school, which is in the UK, applied to the US universities, too. Personally, for me, as an international student, it was a bit of a hassle to apply to the US. There are a lot of great schools and universities in the UK as well.

Do you think many things set the UK application process apart from the US application process?

Take what I say with a pinch of salt because I didn't follow through with the US application. What I've heard from friends and colleagues though is that the US universities are keener on looking at you from a broader perspective. Your extracurriculars are super important; how much volunteering you do is important; and your actual grades, obviously, need to be there as well.

In the UK, on the other hand, you write something called a personal statement. You'll write that depending on where you want to apply. Generally, it is advisable to start doing that maybe at the end of the calendar year of your final year. So if you're in year 13, then it would be around the end of November or so of that year. This part of the application is really big for the UK. They don't concentrate on your extracurriculars. To take that a step further, even Oxbridge, the collective name for Oxford and

Cambridge, is especially just focused on your academic ability and that really shines through their interview processes as well.

Ok, and now that you've graduated, what are some of the career prospects that you seek to accomplish?

That's a really good question, actually. I graduated, as I said, last summer, and I was just very lost. I had no idea. Some people have it figured out, *"I'm going to definitely do this. I'm definitely going to go into law, etc."* — but that just wasn't me. So, I spent a bit of time thinking and trying to dabble a bit in the water to see what was out there.

Now, I've decided to go down the data science route and the data analyst route. I'm actually currently in the middle of filling out massive amounts of applications and appearing for interviews. I had a couple of interviews already this week for those particular positions.

What sort of subjects did you go in for in high school? Did you also take any extra credit courses?

The subjects I took were Maths, Physics, and Chemistry. I didn't take any additional courses in terms of academics.

As far as credits from extracurriculars were concerned, I am really big into rowing. I'm a small person, so I actually sit in the back of the boat and I cox. That's been a massive part of my life. I also did a bit of music as well, not a huge amount, but a bit at school and what's called a pre-U Short course. The CIE Pre is the board I did for Physics and Chemistry but they actually offer an AS level course called the pre-U short course, too; I did that in Spanish. Don't ask me to speak any Spanish please!

Haha, sure. Did you participate in any other competitions or exams?

The school that I went to was really good at pushing their students to enter competitions. I knew I wanted to do something in STEM at the university, so I took the Cambridge Chemistry Challenge and I got a gold in it. I was really happy with it, but then apparently there was a Zirconium or such that ranked above that, which I found out about only later. There were also the Olympiads; I did the Math, Physics and Chemistry ones.

Were you on a student council or holding any leadership roles?

No, I never sat on our student council. There was a debate team and a ton of other things to do. I was mostly focused on the rowing side of things because debate was something that didn't really interest me at all. This is also maybe partly why I didn't want to go into the US system, where they really encouraged having done a lot of that. I knew that I didn't really want to do that so I thought I will just stick to the straight and narrow.

You mention how rowing was an integral part of your life, and you spent a lot of time on it. Were you able to highlight the sport along with your academics well in your application? How do you think that would have impacted their decision on selection while reading the application?

That's an excellent question! A personal statement is, if I remember correctly, about a page long and they're quite strict about the word limit. My very final paragraph which was about eight lines was to do with rowing. So, it was important. As you said, it was a big part of my life, even at that stage, but I deliberately didn't make it a bigger deal (than those eight lines) in the application because I knew that they wanted only a paragraph at the bottom. This was where you got to speak about what your interests are, what your hobbies are, etc. It was just a kind of a formality to see whether you are an interesting person. But the vast majority of the application focused on the stuff that I did at school like academic projects.

A big question I have right now is if at any point you thought you were burning out and how did you avoid that.

I think you have a lot more freedom at university, which is both a good thing and a bad thing. At school, I found it was actually quite easy to stay motivated because there are very clearly set goals by your teachers, usually. You can be relatively motivated. There's also a very clear structure so you go to lessons and there is marked homework. There's tutorials; you're basically guided through the process. This is not to say that it's easy, but I think it's just easier to stay motivated. So the days I wasn't motivated, I stressed myself out by telling myself that I'm going to be told off by the teacher, and that was enough to stay focussed.

At university, I would say it's a completely different ballgame. You're given so much more freedom. You don't have to go to lessons. There are lectures and you aren't forced to attend them. Although you're highly encouraged to go to them, there's not someone who is going to turn around and say, *"Why weren't you at that lecture!"* That freedom may seem really nice to a lot of people, but also it means you have to be so much more aware of how you work. You've to make sure you're not skipping things just because you can skip it for the first time in your life. So, I think that for me was a really important thing to learn in my first year. When you do the other side of things and you're going to do absolutely everything including courses that aren't in your syllabus, you have got to remember what is in your syllabus, what's important and necessary for you to do. So, it's a lot harder at the university.

There are also different kinds of 'not working'. You can still be productive and not working. For me, I just tried to make sure that during my off time, when I was not at the desk, I was still more productive than being unproductive. For instance, productive off time could be like sleeping or participating in a sport or even catching up with friends, but unproductive time makes you almost feel worse. It's those moments of scrolling on your phone that could be bad for you. Also being kind to yourself is extremely important. At school and university, everyone around you is so smart and so driven that you almost can't help but compare yourself to them. It's human nature. I think eventually getting to a point where you're comfortable with who you are and how you're working is almost the goal. The sooner you can achieve that, the happier, the more productive, ironically, you'll be in your next 3-4 years.

That was very helpful. Do you think writing a research paper during High School could make you stand out significantly?

Yeah, for sure. I think if you can write and if you get something published as a high school student, that's insane, right? You'll stand out. I think if you have experience writing in that scientific framework that's just going to be extremely helpful for you once you're at Uni, even if you don't get the paper published. We're obviously talking here about how you get into these universities but the add-on to that is what happens once you're in. Because it's hard to get in but trust me, what happens after that is also very, very hard. Maybe writing now is a really solid idea, and wherever you go, it's going to set you in good stead.

Do you have any tips for the main essay or the personal statement you have to write?

First of all, I'd say the basics. Make sure you're not wasting time by writing something that's way too long because the application goes through UCAS which limits you to a certain number of characters. Just make sure you know the rules. Get your teachers to proofread it, or your friends and family to proofread it. That's all the logistical stuff.

As far as the content is concerned, we've alluded to this quite a few times but make sure that it is quite streamlined towards what you've done academically. For example, if you're lucky enough to have done an internship somewhere, then that's great to put in as long as it's academically focused. Internships don't have to be formal. They can even be something like shadowing a teacher for a summer when they were doing lab work or preparing for a class. Look for as many experiences as you can but make sure when it is towards academia. Why you want to do the subject and what you've already done towards it will help to show them that you can cope with the kind of strenuous intensity that you'll get.

Do you have any advice for the interview stage?

About four in five people are interviewed. The nicest thing that someone told me was that they're not trying to catch you out. I think especially when you're quite young and you go to an interview, you are always thinking they're testing me. Why are they asking this question? Why is it so hard? It is hard, but the other thing isn't really true. Yes, they're assessing you, of course, but they also want to see you, right? They don't want to see how well you'll do when you're super stressed, because you're not going to be super stressed in that way at Uni.

Make sure you know the syllabus, but also try to relax as much as possible. It's a conversation you're having, not one person just asking another person a barrage of questions to test them. If you get stuck, speak out loud. If they ask you some really hard dynamics question, for instance, start jotting stuff down, maybe start by drawing a force diagram, that's always a nice place to start and say, *well, what's gravity doing? Where's the normal reaction going? Which direction is it? Where's the resultant force?* Just think out loud. It sounds so strange, but if you're going down a wrong path, they may be able to see how and they may react much more positively: *"That's interesting. But have you considered this?"* So, it's a lot less stressful for you as well.

I think the worst thing to do is to not say anything and get stuck because then you're just there with a blank piece of paper and a pencil, not writing anything. And they want to help you but can't because they don't know what you're thinking. So even if you have no idea what's going on, think out loud. Make use of the interviewer's presence because they're there to help you. Try to have fun. A good interview should feel like it was really hard but also that you had a great conversation with the interviewer.

What do you think sets the Cambridge interview apart from other college interviews?

I would say that it's quite similar to Oxford, but it's different from the other universities. Cambridge really interviews a lot of people. A lot of universities don't even interview, and those that do, their interview process isn't as long. There are universities like Imperial College London that also have extensive interviews. But in general, I think Cambridge really prides itself on how many people they interview and how seriously they interview everyone. They want to have an idea of how easy it will be to teach and work with this person. I had two interviews with just two interviewers and these details will depend on your course in college. But it'll always be something like that. The reason they do this is that there are these things called "supervisions" at Cambridge and that is very small group teaching. So, they try to emulate those supervisions in the interview setting, which is why they have an interesting interviewing style in the first place. I'd say that that's the main thing that sets Cambridge interviews apart.

Things to Remember

- Focus on academics and activities related to the field of study you want to pursue in the personal statement. The last paragraph can be about you and your hobbies.

- Always make sure to never get stuck and stay silent during interviews. You can think out loud, jot down different ideas, and draw diagrams. Imagine the interview is just a regular conversation with the interviewer.

- Your "off time" can be productive as well. Limit the amount of unproductive "off time".

University of Waterloo:
Harshita Singh Pahwa

Year of graduation: 2023

Major: Mathematical Finance and Statistics

Other universities that were applied to: Universities in the UK, the US, University of Hong Kong (HKU), and Hong Kong University of Science and Technology (HKUST)

High School Programme: Central Board of Secondary Education (CBSE)

What led you to pick Canada compared to the US, UK, and Hong Kong?

I think the biggest reason was that while growing up, I wasn't sure what I wanted to do, but I did know for sure that Math was what I was inherently good at. Interestingly, it also opened a lot of avenues for me. I think the University of Waterloo was one of the better universities when it came to Math, and that's why I ended up choosing it.

When people compare Canada and the US, an important factor is the PR and living in that country. That is definitely a pro but at the same time, we also have a course offering called Co-op, which made me decide one country over the other. Essentially this allows you to study while you work; you study a term and then, you work a term. So I pretty much had the opportunity to dive into different fields while studying. This is a really helpful process in getting clarity on what you want to do in the future.

I did my first two co-ops as a data scientist, and now I'm working in the finance industry. I think there is a lot of exposure that it gives you. I got to work for Nissan as a data scientist and now I'm working for Sun Life Capital Management as a financial analyst for them. It's pretty much like me stepping back from studies every four months. I'm getting the chance to work and then seeing if that works for me.

They allow you to do internships but not just for summer. Is it in the middle of the term?

Yes, also you are working pretty much as a full-time employee. You can choose to do four or eight months at a time. That gives you a lot of time to understand the company itself, the work culture, etc.

And does the university have a set of companies that they tie up with for the co-op programme? Or can you apply to any company of your choice for those 4-8 months?

You have a choice whether to use the university portal or to externally apply to a company of your choice.

The university is tied to a ton of great companies and if you match their job profile, you must take it. Otherwise, you can apply using external job boards.

So, with all the exposure through co-op, what do you see yourself drawn towards in terms of the future?

It was about a year ago that I actually decided what my major would be. So, I came in as an undeclared Mathematics major. Now I'm doing a double major in Mathematical Finance and Stats.

I do like doing pure Math but it isn't something that I see being applied to my life personally. That's why I feel like options that would help merge it with finance, but at the same time using technology would be best for me. Although I am not a CS, I feel like Math puts me in a position to be able to learn all the new things. I want to be able to pick up some sort of computing and put it together with finance and quant.

Sounds very interesting. You said the co-op was a highlight for you in the process of applying to places. Were there any differences that you found in the application itself among the US, UK and Canadian universities?

I did CBSE. I don't think that it really prepares you for getting into a US university per se. There are a lot of extracurriculars involved that CBSE schools often don't pay much heed to. On the other hand, Canadian universities actually do take into consideration your scores. That becomes a little more helpful in your application if you appeared for CBSE, like me. If I remember correctly, the Common App essay was not there in most of the Canadian universities. It was more about what you've done and just putting that on paper rather than putting an essay out. So I think application-wise, it was definitely just more convenient to apply to Canadian universities (not necessarily easier though).

It took me months to write the Common App for the US universities. I didn't have to do that for Canada.

The UK, on the other hand, did have an essay, not the same kind as the US one but I think it was the easiest to write. For me, it was the UK and Canada, and then the US, in ascending order of difficulty.

And what subjects did you take in high school?

I had PCM (Physics, Chemistry, Math). Along with that, I had English and Fine Arts.

What extracurriculars did you do? For a lot of applications, especially to the US, that is very important, right?

From even before high school, I've been very involved in projects related to art. I did a lot of things that led me to the direction of having multiple extracurriculars in that field. Through my US application, I tried to bridge the gap between my artistic abilities and a subject like Mathematics, and I put it together. A lot of that went into my Common App essay. It was a very significant part of my application.

I played basketball in school as well. So, I ended up going to more levels beyond high school like the state level. I had that on my resume as well. That's pretty much the gist of it.

You were drawn to Math and Art you said. I know that a lot of students interested in art look for competitions to participate in to level up. Were there any that you participated in or won that you were able to highlight in your application?

I was a volunteer for a group called The Delhi Street Art. Public defecation is a huge problem in India, so the project picked upon the whole Swachh Bharat Abhiyan theme. We transformed many walls in public spaces into beautiful things. The Delhi Street Art did these several murals all over the city and they did it for beautification. I got involved in that through school.

Would that be considered as community service as well?

It would be. I also did a little bit more for the Swachh Bharat Abhiyan like installing toilets in schools and setting up systems where you teach students within classes about this entire issue. When I was in high school, it was a huge thing. It had just started and we got into it.

So, how did you go about bridging the gap between Art and Math; they're considered two very different things, right?

I feel like there's a lot of beauty in numbers, and it's not just about the artistic process behind it. Do you know that there's this Math problem that says 0.99 is actually equal to 1? If you keep going into the nines, 0.99 is equal to 1. The way to do it is just such a beautiful process of getting to that end. That's an example.

You can also see something like the Fibonacci sequence in plants and flowers around you. I think that is something that was always there. I always had a love for numbers, but I also had this artistic side to me. I don't know if I could bridge the gap, but I was able to draw a lot of such similarities between the two.

Interesting! And did you also hold any leadership positions when you were in high school?

I was in the Student Council for three years, from 9th to 11th Grade. I was also the captain of my school basketball team. During the first year, I was the Assistant Discipline in charge, the next year I was the Sports Captain, and then, the third year, I was a House Captain for my school.

Were you able to take any internships alongside all of these responsibilities in high school during the summer?

Not internships per se. I went to a Counsellor for SAT coaching. They had started a segment where they were guiding CBSE school students for SATs. I don't know if they're still doing it, but initially, when they did begin, I helped them out with teaching the lower-grade students while I was in twelfth.

With all the different things for Math, Art, Basketball, and your voluntary work, how did you go about making sure that you were never falling behind on anything?

It was definitely quite overwhelming because you have to look forward to applying to the university while also maintaining your academic scores. I was in an Indian system where I strongly believe that everyone is very focused on just grades. I was applying to all these international universities with all of these different requirements. So I think that scheduling these definitely became very difficult, to begin with, but after a point, I was able to navigate by rescheduling some of my tasks. You know how on your MacBook you have calendars? I just took a screenshot of every month as it went by and put it as my background. So, I always knew what it was that I had to do.

And I think one thing I picked up – even though it was after I came to the University – was that I always ended my day with the to-do list on the notes app. I would write down everything I had to do the next day from brushing my teeth to taking a nap, everything went into it. I feel like that has helped me over time, putting everything into blocks and doing it in that way.

Would you have any advice for making the actual college profile and the application itself?

I think that a lot of our time goes into stressing about what we should write and what we should put in. Talking to people really helped me. I had an advisor who helped me at the same time. I feel like talking to peers, parents and friends gives you a little more perspective about what you want to do. You don't need to know what you have to do.

Studying in a university abroad does give you the opportunity to switch between majors. I have friends who did two whole years of something, did co-ops, and then decided that that was not their cup of tea. Don't be so stressed about what you think you want to do and where it's going to go. Just do whatever you're doing the best that you can. So just make a profile that you feel proud of. This is a whole new journey after school, just prepare yourself. It's a lot of fun but it's also a lot of work. That's about all I have to say.

Do you have any tips for writing the essay?

That's a difficult one. Don't think about making it too unique because I think we think way too much about it. We think that it has to be such a different story, and that's how we're going to get in. Just write something that makes you feel like you're true to yourself and something that you're proud of. At the end of the day, I don't think the essay is the make-or-break point. It is important but don't overthink it. At the same time, don't not think about it at all.

Things to Remember

☞ The Canadian co-op programme is a great advantage which helps you find your way if you're unsure about the direction you want to go into or the field you want to enter.

☞ Canadian schools give more importance to grades than US schools do. Canadian applications do not require a common app essay.

☞ Have conversations with advisors, teachers, parents, friends who have applied, etc., to broaden your horizon – whether that's to think about extracurriculars or the essays you're going to end up writing.

University of Southern California: Mehak Kapoor

Year of graduation: 2024

Major: Business Administration

Other universities that were applied to: Northeastern, Boston University, UCLA, Emory University, George Washington University, Indiana, Claremont McKenna

High School Programme: International Baccalaureate® Diploma Programme (IBDP)

What sort of career prospects do you see opening up for you?

I would say, right now, I'm a little bit confused as to what field I want to go into particularly. But I'm going to use this year and the next year to do internships to get more clarity. Private equity and venture capital firms are what I'm looking into right now, or even consulting firms. But I'm also really interested in start-ups and entrepreneurship.

I have plans to join clubs at USC in the coming year. There is a big array of clubs that can help you figure out what prospective career pathway you want to get into.

Then over the summer, hopefully, do some internships and see which field I'm interested in.

If you did IB, what were your HLs and SLs?

I actually did GCSE and then I did IB. GCSE is the British curriculum. Within GCSE I took triple Science, English Literature and Language, French, Business, Economics and Psychology. And for IB, I took four HLs. I graduated with Business, Economics, Biology and English Lit Lang HLs, and French and Math SLs.

Wow. 4 HLs must have been a large workload. If you don't mind, could you just share your predicted and final grades?

Yes, sure. Our school predicted one core point. I was predicted a 43, so they had actually predicted a perfect score. I ended up graduating with a 39 because I didn't actually sit the exams. They did it based on IAs and tests that we did throughout the year. I was pretty alright with the 39. The thing that really pushed my application was a perfect score.

And along with the extremely competitive and difficult IB or even during your GCSE, did you do any extra credit scores like AP?

I did two SAT subject tests. I did Math and French.

Do you think actually doing those was a worthwhile use of your time, or do you think that if someone didn't do it, then it wouldn't make that much of a difference?

I think that if you want to be a Business major, a Math subject test plays a really big part. I know I didn't apply as a Business major, but I did the IRGB, which is a double programme with Business and International Relations. I think that having the Math subject test was important for me. The French one I did for fun. I know French quite well, so I winged it. But if you don't have a strong HL and you're going to study Business, I would recommend doing a SAT subject test. I did the SAT and ACT. I dropped the ACT because it just wasn't for me. So, I submitted my SAT scores.

And do you mind sharing how much you got on the SAT?

I ended up getting 1440 with the super score, and 1420 without super scores.

A large part of the US application, besides the SATs, are the extracurriculars, right? So do you mind sharing some of the extracurriculars you did?

Sure. I would say, the main premise of my application outside of grades was a social venture that I took part in. I co-founded this project, which was dedicated towards educating rural girls in Uganda, my birth town, about the importance of feminine hygiene and health. I ran a 4-day workshop and I paired with a charity initiative called Smiles that funded the workshop and distributed reusable sanitary pads for the girls. They also helped raise a lot of hygiene products like soaps. We created pouches with stationery. It was such a huge project that I actually involved my school and the Smiles initiative in it. I think that played a huge part in my admission as well. I also did some internships that probably helped out, too.

Other than that, I ran a Business Club in my school, so showing that business leadership initiative and ability might have worked in my favour. I also did a bit of emceeing.

You mentioned your internships, right? How did you go about getting the internships in the first place? Was it through school or through any personal connections? Or was there any other platform you used to actually get the internships?

As a school-going student, it's really hard to get internships. I would say the first place to look for are personal contacts. I think that those really help the most. One of my internships was through the school. It was actually through one of my teachers in school who had recommended me. I would say that build that connection with your teachers. It's so important because they are happy to help you with things like internships.

Yes, absolutely. Were there any other competitions as well that you were looking out for, during your school?

I took part in the UKMT, which is a Standardised Math Test. I don't think that played a very huge role in my application because I didn't score very high. But I think that just showing that you take part in challenges or rigorous things that challenge your brain or challenge your thinking, I think could actually be good in the application as well. It can really help show that you go out of your way to take part in these competitions. I helped a sneaker startup as well. I was their social media strategist, and I think that was useful in showing that I was working part-time for a bit.

Alright. You already spoke about running a business club. Was there any other sort of leadership role that you highlighted in your application?

I think I forgot to mention, but I was the Deputy Head Girl. I would say that these roles are not groundbreaking. They aren't going to sway their decision. But everything together does show that you're a proactive student. And I think that when you do all these things together, it shows that you can handle school, a leadership role, an internship, and still manage to take initiative towards things that interest you. So, I think that it's important to be an all-rounded individual, and in that sense, it helps. But if you're not the head girl, there's no need to stress about that. On its own, it doesn't contribute to anything.

And I believe something that universities look for might also be community service, in addition to everything you've mentioned. Apart from the project you did, was there any other community service?

I did a lot of CAS work. I took on every opportunity that the school provided. I volunteered at beach cleanups. I did this environment work at an environmental group and did their marketing a little bit to help save the turtles. I also took part in a Ramadan initiatives program that got featured in the newspaper. I'd say these small things just add up and make your application look good. We donated a bunch of meals during Ramadan for the labour workers.

When you're choosing what community service you do, don't just do anything. The universities will definitely see through that when they're reading your application. Do something that is meaningful to you and who you are as a person. I think that because I did my work on time because I'm all about feminism and education, my charity initiative and my ventures were also aligned with that.

But do you think showing so many CAS hours and community service hours actually played a role in your application?

I think it played a very minor role because it's so easy to put in a few hours here and there and then put it on your application. But I think that for it to stand out, it needs to be something unique. Everyone donates food and clothes.

You really need to think out of the box, if you're making community service a major part of your application. You need to think out of the box as to what project you're going to take part in and how impactful that's going to be.

Alright. And did you receive any prizes or awards in school, which you think you highlighted?

Nothing significant. I got those end-of-year awards, for instance, the highest grade in Economics award. I don't think it did much to the application. But if your school offers some significant awards, I think that it makes a difference because a lot of my friends here didn't take honours classes but they definitely did get awards. My school didn't provide too many of those opportunities. I think the universities know that each school will be different. But I'd say, if there are awards in your school, aim for them, because awards can become quite important to your application.

One burning question I've had is how you were able to balance your time throughout all this. You put in so many CAS hours, community service hours, and then also 4 HLs and the heavy school load. How did you manage to balance your time for everything?

That's a good question. I feel like when I was doing it, I didn't think that I was balancing my time. I was always behind, or at least that's what I felt. But it all worked out in the end. I think that it's always quality over quantity. If I'm putting in work to study for my SATs, I'd rather put in two good hours. I'm not going to sit there and study for six hours and burn myself for the next day. I think a lot of people do this. They think that if they pull an all-nighter, they'll be able to finish all the college essays by 4 a.m. But what's going to happen is that the next day, you end up doing zero work, the day after that, you're going to do no work again. You'll be so burnt out from working all those long hours over one day.

Balancing your time is actually key. Just put in 2-3 good hours and dedicate them to one specific thing, whether that's writing the essay or studying for Economics, etc. That was how I navigated through it. I just dedicated a small amount of time each day. That way you're not overwhelmed and when you get overwhelmed, you get burnt out.

Sleep is really important. I never compromised on my sleep; all my friends made fun of me for going to bed at 11 p.m. every day. But that's how I had the energy to pull through the next day.

In addition to these two, I really think that it is important to maintain a good relationship with your teachers because they're actually your biggest asset. Your teachers will help you out so much. Sometimes I would go to my teachers and ask for an extension on a project when I was under a lot of stress, and nine times out of ten, they did say yes. Be on top of your work, but if you feel like you're burnt out, ask for that extension, so that you can do it properly and get a good grade on that project.

How did you actually avoid getting burnt out? Was it just making sure you worked in small breaks or periods of time and making sure you had enough time to yourself?

I would not say that I never got burnt out. I definitely did but I realised that it's actually about prioritising yourself. If nothing is going in your brain at that moment, don't force yourself to study. Just put it away and come back to it later.

College is not any easier, but I promise you, it's a little bit easier than your last two years of high school. When you're studying and when you're going through the whole process, just think that you're going to be set for college. I think that the reason I'm not struggling that much is because I took on so much in high school. Being an international student, you have to take on a lot more. You have to study for SATs, you have to learn the American system, do SAT subjects or do APs. You go out of your way to do that.

You have to apply to all these places; you have to finish IB. And IB is not easy. I'd say two things are important. The first thing to avoid getting burnt out is if you're not feeling good at the moment, don't do it. The second thing is, to take IB if you can take it. It really prepares you for college so well. College is definitely hard, but I don't think it's harder than IB. If you take IB, especially subjects that align with the major you're planning to take, you're so set for college in terms of time management.

Regarding IB, what actually led you towards taking 4 HLs? Do you think highlighting that was actually a big part of your application?

I actually didn't take 4HLs as a strategic move or because I was trying to get into college. I didn't know whether I wanted to take Business or Economics HL. But I knew that I really wanted to take Biology and English Language HLs.

I think having a science subject as an HL shows that you stand out because all business majors will take the standard HLs. I mean, if you can take Math, please take Math HL. I couldn't do it. But if you are good at Math or Science, it is really helpful. I couldn't choose between Business and Economics, but I knew that I really wanted to do both. The workload increased, of course. From Business HL to Business SL wasn't a big deal.

I don't know if taking 4 HLs played a big part, but I think that if they were coming down to two applicants and I was the one with 4 and the other person had 3, they would probably go with the one with 4. Besides, you get more credits in college. I have had more credits than everyone else who took IB because I took 4 HLs.

That makes sense. Do you have any advice or tips for making the college profile and selecting what activities to do?

I guess I've said this but I'll just say it once more. Whatever activity you try to do, try to make sure that it represents who you are as much as possible. Because I know for a fact, that they can tell when someone else is forcing you to do it. Whatever you do, make sure that it comes from you and who you are. At the end of the day, there are so many students with good grades, especially at top colleges, that what they need is that extra edge.

Also, don't make your application extra formal. I didn't. I used exclamation marks in my USC application because there were some fun questions at the end. I made a joke and showed a part of my personality there. I mean grades are important but there comes a point where they feel like everyone has good grades. Now what to do? So, work hard, and get your grades up definitely, but when you're writing your application, don't leave behind the much more human part of you. Display how you're a different person and how you're unique.

And what about the essay - would you have any tips for us for that section of the application?

I did take a gap year, so it's been a while. Because of covid, I decided to take a gap year. I was supposed to be a sophomore, which is why I didn't get the SAT optional benefits. But as far as I remember, I think I wrote four drafts. When I was writing the first one, I had somewhat of an idea. When you're writing the essay, don't just start writing it. Make sure that you have an outline of each paragraph. Like each paragraph should have an idea because you have to make each paragraph interesting and the top and the bottom of the essay need to be super inspirational. They need to be linked to each other.

It can't just be random like *I'm good at this. I'm good at this. And I'm good at this.* It needs to link and it needs to have a kind of a storyline. It must be emotive for sure. Because they read so many applications that they're just waiting for that one that's going to tingle their emotions or make them feel like, *oh, wow, this is great!*

Things to Remember

- Build a strong relationship with your teachers so that they can help and mentor you. Don't be shy to ask for an extension on assignments.

- Be selective about what activities you perform for community service. They should be in line with who you are as a person and what you believe in, otherwise, colleges will be able to see through your application.

- Don't be shy to express your individuality in essays. Almost everyone has good grades. You need to show that you are unique. Some humour, etc., will help you set yourself apart.

Imperial College London: Jay Rameshwar

Year of graduation: 2023

Major: Biomedical Engineering

Other universities that were applied to: MIT, Stanford, Johns Hopkins, Purdue, University of Maryland, Harvard University, Yale University, among others.

High School Programme: N/A

When you were applying to various universities, except for the fact that one application worked for five different schools in the UK, what were some of the other differences in the application process between the US and the UK?

I think the US takes a more holistic approach to admissions. I think obviously test scores and GPA are important, but they also have essays that are more subjective. They look at the overall profile of the candidate. They didn't really have a specific section per se to talk about my research. They asked questions that were a bit more subjective. So, you get 650 words to talk about something you enjoy doing outside of school or the time you were challenged with something. They ask very interesting questions and they learn about you as a person.

The UK does that as well. But I think there's a bit more of an emphasis on your classes in the UK and the test scores you've received. In my UK application, they had a 2,000-word essay that was pretty dense. In that essay, I talked about my motivations for pursuing research. The focus was on the type of research I did, what I learned from it, and what exactly my work entailed. In particular, for the UK you don't apply to a university, you apply to a specific course. So I applied for engineering at all the schools I had reached out to in the UK. I could really tailor my application for someone interested in engineering.

Whereas with the US schools, you apply to the school itself. You can apply directly to the School of Engineering, and that's what I ended up doing for most of the US applications I filled out.

Essentially, in the US you have to highlight your full profile with extracurriculars but in the UK, you've to highlight mainly the test scores, your grades and your academic performance.

Exactly, and, in particular, they had asked questions about my research experience. For example, for Imperial College London, where I eventually ended up getting accepted, they had a few stages of interviews. In the first stage, they had a skills-based interview. A member of the faculty asks questions about your background and about Math and Science topics that you've covered in high school. They try to get an understanding of the level you're at. They also have an admissions exam. I had to take a short exam prior to getting that interview. That was very different from any US Schools.

US schools didn't really have an academic interview per se or a skills-based interview. The interviews are again more holistic. They ask about your interests and how you spend your time outside of school as opposed to directly focusing on your academics.

And what do you plan to do in the future? Are you going to work in the UK? Have you decided anything like that?

I hope I have career prospects, fingers crossed. I think I'm in the process of decision-making right now, but I see it bifurcating in two paths. One path I'm looking at right now is research. That's something I'm interested in and I've done it in high school. I recently got published. It was my first publication in a scientific journal, so that's a big accomplishment for me. I think, building on that, I'd like to apply for grad schools and possibly pursue a PhD. Whether that's in the UK or the U.S, I haven't made up my mind.

The other path I'm looking at is applying to biotech companies or startups within the biotech field. Eventually, that's where I see myself working, i.e., in biotech, and pursuing research in that field. I think it'll be contingent upon which opportunity I find best once I graduate.

I guess I'm still figuring things out. As far as the UK versus US goes, I love being in the UK; it's been an amazing experience. But I think, ultimately, I do see myself returning to the US.

Alright, and what subjects in high school helped you strengthen your understanding of the area you were looking to major in?

I went to high school in the US. I did all my schooling in the US. I had a pretty varied amount of subjects including AP US History and AP World History, AP English and AP Language Arts. But I also took all my science courses like AP Chemistry, AP Physics, AP Biology and AP Calculus. I had a strong interest in languages, so I took AP Spanish during my junior year, and AP Chinese during my senior year.

May I ask how much you got in the AP classes?

Yeah. Calculus, Chemistry, Biology and Physics were all 5s. Unfortunately, I got a 4 on the Physics C Electricity and Magnetism; it used to be my strongest suit back in high school. Then I got a 5 on AP Spanish, which I was very proud of, 5 on AP English and AP World History. Chinese is a very tough language, so I think I got a 3 eventually on that.

Did you also take any honours classes or extra courses related to these?

Yes, I think during the freshman sophomore year, there were many AP course offerings. In freshman year, I took Honours Biology and honours Precalculus. It was in sophomore year that I started taking the AP equivalents, my junior and senior years. Because I took two languages throughout High School, I could do a bit of an accelerated path. Normally people take AP Physics 1 and then get to Physics C. I skipped AP Physics 1 and went directly to Physics C. And people take honours Chemistry and then get to AP Chemistry. I skipped the honours and went straight to AP. This was mainly because I took both Spanish and Chinese in high school. It was a great experience but now looking back, I think it also made my high school experience quite tough. It was a huge course load I had taken on.

How do you think being a multilingual student impacted your application for both the US and the UK?

In the UK I don't think they have too much of an emphasis on your ability to speak other languages. But I think in the US, it was nice to have that. It's a black box really—who gets in and who doesn't get in. So, I can't really point to one specific thing and say, *that's the reason I got in! or I didn't get in!* I'm sure it helps. But if you have to sleep two hours a night because you have to take an AP Spanish and

AP Chinese course, then I wouldn't recommend it. I think I definitely enjoyed taking both those languages but one thing I had to do was to balance. That's why the accelerated Science and Math courses. In hindsight, it would have been a little bit better for me to drop the course load, and maybe pick things in a different way.

And apart from all the APs and Honours, what extracurriculars did you do? Because you had to have that in your US application, right?

I was always very interested in debate; I like to think of myself as a pretty eloquent and well-spoken guy. So, I did debate for all four years in high school. I was the captain of my team in senior year. I was also into Math and I competed in the American Math Competition. I was on my high school's Math team and went to Math team meets throughout school. I was the captain in my senior year.

I also played soccer and squash. I was on the varsity squash team in my junior and senior years. Beyond that, I did some volunteer work. In middle school, I was part of a club called the Fairfield Enrichment Club. It was for very passionate students in Middle School who wanted to pursue Math and Science competitions and you would essentially go to classes that were student-run. High school or college students would be teaching middle schoolers Math concepts to prepare them for competitions in middle school. So I was a student there in middle school initially.

Once I was in high school, I was offered the opportunity to actually teach, so it went full circle.

Cramped summer, I interned at the Multiple Myeloma Research Foundation, which is a cancer research organisation based nearby. My work there was more like data analysis and keeping track of the clinical trials that were running. Then in my junior year, I was accepted into Yale Discovery to Cure Program, which is a selective programme for high school summer research they run. I live in Connecticut so New Haven wasn't too far. I was able to commute there during the summer to work. In my senior year, I returned for my senior internship and that was a very rewarding experience. I made a great connection and relationship with the Professor there, Dr Braddock. Now, in college during covid, I opted to take a gap year, so I was able to return to his lab during the year. I took on an independent project and that's how I received this publication.

I was just wondering why this line is so cramped did. How were you able to? How did you balance your time with the heavy course load, the extracurriculars you were doing, and the volunteer work?

Something that really helped me in high school was having a good routine. I knew exactly when my classes would begin and finish. I knew what days I would have Math team practice or debate team practice and where the tournaments were. I think having a good schedule and picking things you're really interested in would be it.

I really enjoyed being in the Math team and the friends I made in the Math team. When I go back to my hometown for breaks, I still hang out with them and meet up with them. I'm still in touch with them. It's the same for the debate team, my volunteer work, and my research experience.

I think if you're passionate about something and you pursue it, you can find time to do everything. And obviously, in junior year and senior year, there are a ton of exams and AP tests, and you have to prepare for everything, it becomes tough to balance everything. I think that's when you have to prioritise and pick the things that really matter to you. That might mean dropping one or two things. There would be a season where I wasn't playing soccer, and I wasn't going to all the tournaments for squash. It's not ideal but you've got to sometimes pick and choose what you can actually do and what you can't.

Right, so, how did you avoid getting burnt out? A lot of students put themselves under pressure and pick up a lot of things and, then, they end up getting burnt out at the end.

I experienced burnout once I got into college. I think in high school, I was very focused. I wanted to get into a good university, and eventually, the decision came down to Vanderbilt University, UC San Diego in the US, and Imperial College London across the ocean in England. And I think I was very motivated to get into a good college. That kept me going for the most part.

Another big part of that was that I did enjoy everything I was doing. I made some really good friends at all my classes and I think particularly in junior year, there's almost some camaraderie in how much work everyone is doing. Everyone's really striving to get a great college and work really hard in school to maximise the chances of that happening. I think surrounding yourself with people who put the similar mindset forward, who are all working towards the same thing, helps. It helped me sometimes. I tend to be a bit competitive, but I'm very lucky that my friends were very supportive throughout high school. We would all help each other with our homework and preparation for exams. I think at the end of the day, I was very motivated to build the best possible application I could. I did everything I could to make sure that happened.

And as for the standardised tests, did you take the SAT or the ACT?

I took the SAT and I got a 1570 out of 1600. It was out of 1600 at the time that I took it. I took the PSAT and I was a National Merit commended student.

So, you got a scholarship, right?

No, unfortunately, it's one step below.

Ah, okay. Still, it's phenomenal. And did you receive any prizes or awards in school?

Oh, yes. My school has an award ceremony at the end of every year. In my junior and senior years, I got awards for pursuing languages and for my performance in the language courses. I got an award for science for my performance in my biology class. And in my senior year, I was the high scorer on the American Math Competition for my school. So, I received an award for that. Off the top of my head, those are the three main ones that I can remember.

Did you qualify for the AIME (the prestigious American Invitational Mathematics Exam)?

Yes, in my senior year I did. But I didn't do anything after that.

Finally, I'd like to ask you if you have any advice for profile-building for US universities.

I think if you're interested in applying to a US school you have to build a well-rounded application with extracurriculars, academics, and your interests. I think at the end of the day you have to pursue things you really care about. You have to pick things you enjoy. If you're interested in them, you'll perform better at them, and you'll be more dedicated towards them. I wouldn't recommend picking a bunch of things just because they look good on your application. I know that can definitely seem like the right way to go about things. But I think if you don't do well in them, or if it's clear that you're only here to tick a box, it doesn't translate well into how your application comes across.

The second thing is, I think a lot of people stress out in high school. I know it is about getting into a good college. It's easy for me to say now because I'm on the other end of the process, but it will always work out in the end. Even if you don't get into the dream school you wanted to get into in high school, you can perform well in college and get into the dream career you want.

At the age of 20, you're only in the first quarter of your life. Who thinks they've lost the game in the first quarter? You have to stay at it and keep fighting for things you're interested in and put effort into them. Learn how to stay disciplined.

One thing I realised when I was in high school was that I was very motivated to get to college. Now that I'm in college, I know I have to keep fighting. If you're only thinking a few years down the line, that's probably not enough motivation to keep you happy and satisfied for the rest of your life. You have to find things that are more meaningful and have a deeper desire or drive to pursue them. I know it's hard to do when you're in high school and you just feel like this is your only focus. Once you're in college, I think it becomes a little bit easier to figure out what kind of a person you are and what you want to pursue. I guess my overall advice would be to find things you are really passionate about and pursue them. I understand finding your passion is a big task, but at least you'll have some level of routine and discipline to keep going day to day and keep trying out new things. Finding something you really want to do, I would say, is almost if not more valuable than learning something you don't want to do.

And the last question for today, what advice would you give for the essay?

I think in the UK, you only have one essay and you submit that to all the schools you apply to. So, you have to pick a subject you're interested in studying because you're applying for that specific course, that specific subject. Just make sure your essay builds a coherent profile of your academics, extracurriculars, research, etc., towards that specific subject.

Whereas in the US, if you're applying to the School of Arts and Sciences somewhere, you don't have to have a super coherent application. You're not applying for one specific subject. You can have a more varied application and talk about all your interests. Obviously, it helps to declare something specifically, something you're super interested in. But I think for the US essay, the prompts are laid out broadly enough. I think that what really helps is to take a few days, sit down, and read through the essay prompts. Don't even write anything, just read through the prompts. Think about what the question is asking and how you can best answer.

Colleges have admission meetings where they talk to the students who are looking to apply and discuss prospective students they're looking for and how the application process works. One thing I learned through the process when I attended such meetings from these colleges was that these people who read your applications read dozens of applications a day. If you sound like every other high school student, you're not going to really stick out to them. Really try and focus on what makes you unique as opposed to what you think the rest of the people are doing right. Pick things that are really unique to you. If you start thinking about it a little bit earlier and start developing a good profile for yourself and pursuing things you enjoy, I think it's an easier path to go down.

Things to Remember

- ☞ Find an overarching goal apart from getting into college.

- ☞ Find something that makes you unique and really focus on that in the essays to stand out.

- ☞ Surround yourself with people who have the same mindset so that you drive each other forward. It helps to avoid burnout and makes high school easier.

- ☞ Don't try to do everything. Instead, find things you are passionate about and devote sufficient time and attention to them

Pratt Institute: Naaz Khan

Year of graduation: 2025

Major: Industrial Design

Other universities applied to: UT Austin, Northeastern, CMU, Parsons, UIUC, UCs

High School Programme: International Baccalaureate® Diploma Programme (IBDP)

Industrial design is a discipline that has a lot of interesting scope today for those passionate about visual arts. If I may ask, could you share with the readers what all it entails, if they were to take it up, and what doors it would open for them?

Industrial design is a very broad major and industry. But to keep it simple: it's very similar to the idea of product design since you are essentially engaging in problem-solving for a specific target audience. Therefore, it allows you to think creatively since you are ideally trying to build something.

This makes it super hands-on, which is what I love about it. Industrial design can also be broken down into different parts. For example, you may want to go into shoe design, furniture design, toy design, etc.

Ah, got it. And what sort of career prospects are you looking at pursuing?

I don't really have any solid plans yet. But I do have plans of pursuing a Master's to specialise in a subject within this area itself, once I complete my Bachelors in Industrial Design.

At an IB school — that's The International School, Bangalore (TISB) for you — that comes with the option of choosing HLs and SLs—which subjects did you decide to take up that helped you move closer to the degree?

For my HLs, I took Economics and Math. There are two types of Math subjects that they offer: Applications and Interpretations is one of them, and Analysis and Approaches is the other. I also took Art as an HL. As far as SLs are concerned, I took Physics, English Literature and Language, and Spanish Ab Initio.

Ok, that's interesting. A lot of students think that they should take DT (Design Tech) HL or Art HL if they want to go to an art university. How necessary do you think that is?

Personally, I don't think it is necessary because quite a few people studying at Pratt didn't take any of those.

I think it's more of a personal choice. However, I would recommend it because that way you can also cover your portfolio pieces. It helps you work on two things at once, if you get the right guidance.

With IB, Pratt didn't take any credits for art as a subject. But I think you do get credit if you do AP Art because there are quite a few people here from the US who went to art high schools or they did AP Art. I would recommend it, even if it weren't compulsory to take it.

Did you always know you wanted to pursue this? Did you take Art in 9th and 10th grades as well and was that helpful for the decision-making process?

I did take Art in ninth and tenth grades. I always knew that I wanted to do something related to Art. I took that subject as a way to continue enjoying engaging with it. That's why I also took that forward in 11th and 12th. There's no right or wrong answer, I think. It's up to you and what you want. Take it if you want more experience in art, and want to keep at it, and keep improving.

Could you tell us a little bit more about your portfolio? What sort of requirements did you have? Were there a specific number of pieces they wanted you to complete?

Before I begin, I just want to say covid affected how much work I could actually put in because coming to school and working on art was really important. But most of 11th grade was at home for me. So, I didn't get enough time and I don't think I put in enough effort, I'm going to be honest. That's why when I submitted my application for IB, the work overlapped with my portfolio-building. I had about 10 to 12 pieces. Because it was for IB, I had one recurring theme, which was freedom versus restriction.

With IB, they want to see a range of mediums being used because you're trying to show how much you know, and how in tune you are with what you're doing. This can vary from university to university though. The UK universities wanted to see more major-specific academic work that you've done. The US art universities on the other hand just wanted to see your skill. I think each university demands different things. For example, RISD is really focused on sketching–not just still lifes but figure drawing as well. They look at your technique more than anything. While other universities allow you to apply with whatever work you think you've done best.

I applied to Industrial Design here at Pratt, but if you look at my work, not a lot of it directly relates to Industrial Design. I have paintings, sculptures, a few sketches here and there, and a few still lifes. I showcased a range of everything in my portfolio to show what I'm good at and what I enjoy doing. I also tried to incorporate some digital work there.

See what each university requires. I applied for one of the digital media art courses at UCLA, which was super competitive. They had given four different objectives that you had to achieve with each piece. They give you one theme like 'Redesign a book cover', and then you have to make something related to that. For some universities like UT Austin and CMU, I had to make a video showcasing my work. There can be different demands from universities and you need to figure that out.

But I will say that you should separate your IB work from your portfolio. They can of course overlap. If you have the time, put in more effort so that things don't look forced just because you had something that vaguely fit the theme or prompt or requirement of the university.

When did you start working on your portfolio?

I think 11th grade only, but I would highly, highly recommend starting before. Just start doing whatever art you can at an early stage because you can still combine things together. You can still experiment but at least you have an ample supply of artworks. Then you can put in based on what each university wants. This is what I saw on YouTube where people had a bunch of artworks ranging from different media. Based on what each university wanted, they submitted that. I didn't have the option to do that. But if you do use your time well, and if you plan things well and put in the effort, you can do a good job and make a good portfolio.

Can you use some of the 9ᵗʰ and 10ᵗʰ grade artworks as well in your portfolio, if they're good enough?

At first, I thought that I would do that, but then I saw the change in my work and my progress. I felt that my 11ᵗʰ and 12ᵗʰ grade work was a lot more refined than the 9ᵗʰ grade one. But I wouldn't say don't put it in. If that works for you, then that's completely ok. Some universities want to see your sketchbook pages, and your experimentation, more than the finished pieces. In that case, I used some of my 9ᵗʰ and 10ᵗʰ work. If it was good, then I submitted that.

Understood! And what are some of the extracurriculars that you did during high school?

I tried to do a range of things. During covid, I helped my neighbour raise money for some stray dogs to get some food and vaccines for them. I sold a couple of paintings for this. My art proved to be of some use there.

I also did an internship at a small startup and worked on graphic design to familiarise myself with programmes like Photoshop and After Effects.

In school, I became the Art Prefect, but I don't think a lot happened with that. In terms of extracurriculars like community service, I used to go to a children's home once a week back in 10ᵗʰ Grade. I was meeting kids and teaching art. If you do sports, that's one thing that universities really like. I didn't do sports, but I spoke about my interest in dance, where there was a gap in sports.

Regarding your internship, I was just wondering how you went about getting that internship. Did you know someone who got that for you or was there a platform that you used that helped you connect with companies to get the internship?

My dad knew someone. It was connected with a company that he works in. Thankfully, I had the opportunity to do that. In terms of places that offer internships, I don't have a lot of knowledge of that. In addition to the internship, I also did a film summer programme and animation. Those helped me as well.

So, I guess it ties into visual arts more broadly.

Exactly. Anything related to that I tried to pursue.

I see my classmates right now, and they have three to five assignments every week or are due soon. How did you avoid getting burned out with all the art assignments? And how did you manage to balance your time between art and IB and extracurriculars?

I struggled with time management, and I am still struggling even in university. I feel like I'm just doing art every single day. Sometimes it gets so overwhelming because you have an assignment due and then you finish it and then you have another one. I think you just need to start early with your work. I know this is common advice but it cannot be stressed enough.

I heard that from my seniors too, and I always thought, *"Yeah yeah, I'll do it,"* but I never did, and then only later on realised that I should have taken that advice seriously. In terms of managing IB, allocate a certain time you dedicate to doing art and be on top of whatever assignments your teacher gives you; literally, complete it and do a good job. Even if it means staying up at night and getting less sleep, it's fine. That's the reality; get the work done. That prevents you from getting any backlog. And more than anything, you can always rework it. If you have something to show, you can always come back to it but make sure it doesn't get pushed behind. I remember in 11th grade, at the beginning of IB, the classes were online. Doing art at home just wasn't great. So my friend and I would decide that we're going to do art every day, but we would always push it to the end of the day and not complete anything because we had other essays to write. So we would be prioritising the other side of things.

With IB, there's so much and as an art student, it does get difficult. But I feel like if you plan your time and look at art as something that you enjoy, and if you actually enjoy it, giving time to it wouldn't be an issue. And again, having art and doing it in school makes the biggest difference ever. I did enjoy art a lot in 9th and 10th when I was doing it in school because everyone was around. We were helping each other. I was actually getting work done. Supplies were there and there was a good community, and then 11th and 12th were just at home all alone.

Do you have any tips for making the college profile in general?

Our school made us start working on the Common App super early. If your school doesn't do that, then take the initiative on your own, I would say. They had us make accounts by the end of 11th grade. Have a general idea of what you would like to major in and then go and check out the specific universities you would like to attend. Look at universities that have good programmes for the major you plan to take up. Compare and contrast. Weigh out the factors that really matter to you — whether it's university life, or how strong your major is, the location if you have family around. For me, the most important thing was the major: what they offered as a university and how that may take me forward in terms of career, getting jobs in the future, and internships. Then you make your tentative list.

I think the Common App has six questions. Pick a question that would really showcase who you are as a person and that tells your story to the university. They read so many applications all the time, so you need to make sure yours is memorable and stands out to a certain extent. The university-specific essays require a lot of research. So make an Excel sheet or note it in a Word document where you have all the details of the university. For example, the professors in your major, certain locations on campus, the extracurriculars that they offer, their classes that you would probably be interested in. All of that comes into the "why?" part of the essay. I think Northeastern University wanted an essay on why I wanted to apply to the College of Art and Design. I spoke about my achievements and my interests which were representative of my creative inclination. This whole process requires a lot of research. So, I would say make those Excel sheets and Word documents, whatever may help you stay organised.

The sooner you start, the better because I'm not joking when I say that the workload gets super intense if you're doing IB. I feel like if you're doing another course, it's not too bad. But with IB, all you're doing is writing essays, so take the opportunity to take time in understanding yourself. By the end of it, I feel like you'll look back and be able to say *"Oh, this was kind of fruitful,"* or, *"Oh, I learned something about myself."* All the writing will require a lot of drafts and reworking, and I'm sure teachers help with that. I remember we had a college counselling department that really helped us with it. As a student, you will have to reach out to teachers for it. Don't be afraid to put yourself out there and get guidance from them early on.

For your letter of recommendation, did you go to your art teacher? Does it matter if the letter of recommendation is from someone related to the major that you're applying to?

I don't remember what my school said about it as such, but I feel like it's up to you. At the end of the day, it's the teacher telling the university how good a student you are. I had three teachers that I got recommendations from. I was not allowed to read their recommendations but I got my Math teacher, my English teacher, and my Art teacher, obviously. Some universities only needed one letter of recommendation, and some of them didn't even need one. For those places, I just submitted my art recommendation letter because it was major-specific. I assumed that my teacher would have spoken something about my skill, which was important, and also, who I am as a student.

Things to Remember

- ✒ Each university has different requirements for portfolios and it is important to research and tailor the portfolio accordingly. She also recommended taking art subjects in high school to build up the portfolio and gain more experience.

- ✒ It is important to have a portfolio that showcases a range of mediums and media. If you are in the IB course, try not to let your university art pieces and IB coursework pieces overlap. This way your portfolio can be more tailored towards the various universities' requirements.

- ✒ UK art universities look for more major-specific pieces in the portfolio whereas US art universities try to gauge your overall skills as an artist in a range of mediums.

Emory University: Vihaan Shah

Year of graduation: 2027

Major: Business Administration

Other universities that were applied to: Northeastern University, Boston University, UCLA, Emory University, George Washington University, Indiana University, and Claremont McKenna

High School Programme: International Baccalaureate® Diploma Programme (IBDP)

Did you apply to the UK at all or only the US?

Yes, I did apply to the UK but I withdrew my applications because I sent an ED (Early Decision) to Emory University.

A QUICK NOTE

↬ An early decision ('ED') is a binding application submitted early to one university of your choice. Generally, the deadline for an ED is November 1st, but this could vary from college to college/ university to university.

↬ An ED may help increase your chances of admission a little more because a university gets an assurance that it can admit you (since the application is binding). The applicant is likely to hear the university's decision in January.

↬ If you get into your ED, you must withdraw your applications to other universities (like Vihaan had to do).

↬ There is also something called an Early Action ('EA'), which is like the early decision, except it is not binding. You can send an EA to as many universities/colleges as you want.

↬ Apart from this, you might also hear of something called a Restrictive Early Action ('REA'), which is also non-binding. However, if you apply for an REA at a university, then you cannot apply for EA or ED anywhere else.

To pursue a major like Business Administration, what subjects did you take in high school?

In IGCSE, I had taken English Language and Literature, Coordinated Science (which is a double credit and is compulsory), International Math, Additional Math, Economics, Spanish, and Computer Science. Once I moved to IB, I took Math, Physics and Economics at HL and I took Business, English Lang/Lit, and French ab initio at SL.

How do you think the workload was for you? I've heard that taking Physics and Math at HL can be tough.

In terms of workload, I had done Additional Math, so that helped. I tend to find Physics harder because Math is something that comes more naturally to me. In general, I'd say at least for me at Hill Spring, there was a decent amount of work, but if you are able to manage your time, it's alright. People say that they would pull all-nighters. I have slept every single night and I have taken relatively harder subjects. It is manageable but you just have to know how to go about it.

Also, do you think UK universities lean towards A-level students or IB students?

There's no specific thing. You could have done your education from an Indian board like the ISC or CBSE and it's completely fine.

And for the US, is there a preference like this?

It's the same for the US; there's no specific preference. You'd see A-level people or CBSE students get into the same universities as some of our IB friends get in. In terms of the preparation though, I'd say IB prepares you more in general because it's very rigorous.

What about any competitions or exams such as Olympiads or APs? Did you take part in any of those?

I've given a few Math Olympiads. In fact, I had organized one as well: the first one which was called HSMO (Hill Spring Math Olympiad). I didn't give any APs.

Do you think it's required for a student to take APs?

It's not. It's good if you want to give it; there's no harm in it, you just learn more in general. Sometimes counsellors insist you take it, even though it's really not required.

A big question for students is always about the extracurriculars. You had earlier mentioned streamlining extracurriculars according to the major one is planning to take could be an important step. Could you walk us through some of the extracurriculars that you did throughout high school and the ones that you think made you stand out?

One of the things I mentioned earlier was the Math competition. The interesting thing about that was that it was Hill Spring's first and it was an international one, so it was on a pretty decent scale.

The second would be my own startup, which focuses on helping students get internships, and we are a team of around 20-25 students. Not everyone has access to the same opportunities to work and that's why we started this. It taught me about leadership and responsibilities.

In addition to this, I played golf. During covid, golf caddies didn't have any income because the golfers hadn't been playing, so I helped vaccinate them. I've also been playing the keyboard since second grade and a few of us formed our own band. I've been playing at the annual day since sixth grade every year and it's also helped me raise money through fundraiser events for different things. Finally, I did some peer tutoring from school for the NHS (National Honors Society), which is a US-based society for high schoolers, they have branches in different schools.

So, the last things you mentioned were part of your community service?

Yes.

You also mentioned internships. I was wondering how you spent your Summers? Did you attend summer school?

I think sometimes summer school may not be too helpful. It's just a lot of money that you have to spend.

Really?

Yes, I mean, it doesn't matter too much, especially considering that you spend a lot to go for these. Of course, the experience is good but you're going to eventually experience it in another year or two anyway. I personally didn't attend them. I have a few friends who did and they might have a different opinion.

In terms of internships, I did an internship every summer from grade 9 to 12. They were all at different companies. The last one was more research-oriented. The first four helped me gain work experience in the field of Finance itself. The last one was when I wrote an investment thesis with an analyst. It was for a company's stock and was around 30-35 pages long.

Did you get the investment thesis published?

I didn't get mine published. It can take some time and effort to do that. Universities know that if you're an 18-year-old without external help, it can be difficult to publish it. So, I didn't really spend a lot of time getting it published. But when I was asked to submit it to a few colleges, I submitted it through the common application.

Ok, and do you think publishing a research paper would actually help you stand out or not that much?

There's no harm in publishing it. There are a few people that you can work with, like professors, who can actually help you get it published. That way the publishing becomes relatively easier. There is no such thing that if you have a paper published, you have more chances, and if you don't, your chances of getting into your dream college are low.

I was also interested to know if apart from founding a company, you took up any specific leadership roles in school.

Through school, I didn't do much in leadership, only the Math competition, where I was the co-founder with a few of my friends, and the NHS bit that I mentioned. But I wasn't part of the student council or anything.

Do you think it's a big deal if you become the President or the Head Girl or Head Boy of your school?

In B. D. Somani International School, which is where I studied till 10th grade, it happens through voting. It's definitely good if you're the President because it would reflect that you helped organise things and, in the process, learnt things. It's a good position to have. People should definitely try for it. And more than for the college application purpose, I think just for the learning experience, they should.

What about letters of recommendation? Did you get your teachers to write you any? Do you think the letters had an impact on your application?

One thing to know is that you will never get to see your letter of recommendation. That's like a confidential thing.

I don't know how much it impacts your application because having a good LOR is always better for your application. Accordingly, choose teachers whose subjects you feel you have a better connection with or those that can write you a good LOR, who have worked with you maybe. Some people might say you should get one letter from your English teacher but there's no set thing, no fixed formula like that.

You have to submit two from your school teachers. It sometimes depends from college to college. But you have to submit minimum one, maximum two sometimes, or they can allow you to submit more. Sometimes students even ask 3 teachers to write for them.

In terms of external recommendation letters, I got my golf coach to write me one, and I got the person that I wrote my investment thesis with to write another. I had four in total. Sometimes you might want to submit external ones so wherever it is allowed, you can do that.

Interesting. Would you have any tips for managing and balancing time for all of this?

Make a timetable.

Did you use any tools for that?

Schools give you your respective email IDs. I'd say go on that and make a timetable. If you prefer writing, write it down. If it's on Outlook, you get reminders. For example, in 30 minutes you have to do this. Sometimes in IB you have free blocks, and you end up chilling with your friends. It's great to hang out with your friends, I'm not saying don't do that. I never compromised on any of that but you should also get work done.

I think it depends on your own specific workload as well. Figure out a good balance. Don't compromise on your sleep a lot. If you have to compromise on going out, you can still do that but not on your sleep because then your next day also gets affected.

Do you have any tips for making a college profile and choosing the extracurriculars?

It's good to do things, but you shouldn't specifically do things only for colleges. That is one thing I have learnt. You should genuinely enjoy doing it. Don't do it with the mindset that I'm doing it, so that I can put it on my application, so that I can get into a good college. Because you also want to look genuine.

In terms of your essay, try to be a little different because they read so many essays. When they read yours, they should be like, *oh I read an essay about this!*

I think a lot of it is also based on luck, i.e., who reads your application. One thing through all this is to keep your grades up because that's important. In terms of how much to do, I'd recommend not to do a thousand things. Just do 3-4 things, but do those three four things properly.

That has way more impact than you putting your hands in every single dish possible.

I was wondering if you had any tips for the essays, i.e., when to start writing them. How do we go about starting them? How many drafts did you have to go through before the final one?

The only essay that you can realistically write before the 12th grade starts is your Common App essay. Get that done, get it out of the way because that's important and you have the time. You don't have school because the colleges release their essays after school starts.

Are there different prompts?

Oh, yes. I'm talking about the US one here.

One more thing is to finish off, in fact, would be the IAs. I think I was able to do this well because once school starts, they're going to give you a few tests because they too have to predict your scores. You'd want to finish off your IAs because you have to manage your tests, IAs, and your essays. And you can't compromise on any one of them because your IAs and tests make up your predicted grade and your essays go to the University. Manage these things, well, it'll be fine.

Things to Remember

☞ Utilise the summer of 11th grade well to complete drafts of your Common App so that you have more time to work on it. If you are a part of the IB program, try to also complete your Internal Assessments (IAs) so that you have sufficient time to study for tests in 12th grade.

☞ For LORs, choose teachers whose subjects you feel you have a better connection with. Try to get in a couple of external LORs as well, if possible.

☞ Try to focus your time on only 3 to 4 different ECs, but make sure they are done well and for a sustained period. Their impact is better than doing a thousand things together.

University of British Columbia: Leah Divecha

Year of graduation: 2027

Major: Psychology.

Other universities that were applied to: University of Ottawa, McGill, UBC and Wilfrid Laurier

High School Programme: Indian Certificate of Secondary Education and International Baccalaureate® Diploma Programme (IBDP)

Congratulations on making it to UBC! How was it navigating through the admissions for the university? Were you looking at applying to Canada specifically?

I'm a Canadian citizen so it made sense for me to just apply to Canadian universities. I got scholarships from three of the four universities that I applied to (York University, University of Ottawa, and UBC). I didn't get into McGill but I did get into UBC.

The Canadian application process seems much easier as well when compared to the US or UK ones. I had to write just two essays. I know the US ones require way more.

For Canada, it's mostly one Common App where you put your basic information, your grades, and your extracurriculars. They didn't ask for any other essays or anything like that. UBC was the only school I had to write an essay for.

So, I'd like to start by asking you what board you took for high school. IB, ICSE?

I was in ICSE, and then I went to IB following that.

Okay and did you find the transition difficult? Because I know a lot of students in ICSE consider between A levels and IB.

It definitely was a little strange. Especially having to transfer through the pandemic. You definitely have to like work at it.

And in terms of the syllabus, and stuff like that was the difference between what you covered as an ICSE student and what people would have had as an IGCE student and IB student?

It's definitely that is it not just in the syllabus, but also in the whole learning process. We learn things so differently. There's definitely a difference.

Do you think that was an advantage or disadvantage for you going into IB?

Um, maybe a little bit of both because I know in ICSE we focused a lot more on kind of rote learning and in IG

(Cambridge International General Certificate of Secondary Education) I feel like it's a little bit different. So I think there are some advantages and some disadvantages to that.

Okay, cool. I would just like to ask you what subjects you took in IB.

So I took theatre, HL, English language, HL and psychology HL and Spanish Abinitio. Math SL and biology SL.

And you were in ICSE and switched to IB in high school. Apart from the already rigorous programme that IB is, what were the other things that you were trying to juggle and make time for?

So, Canada luckily doesn't require SATs, so I didn't have to prepare for that. But I've been playing the violin and piano since I was six, so I had a lot of music going on.

Tell me more about that. Did you also have to take music exams and certifications from music schools like Trinity?

So, the music school that I work with is the Symphony Orchestra of India. We work with the Russian system. We don't actually have any levels or grades like the ones that are conducted by Trinity.

We had a whole bunch of concerts. I went to Bangalore to perform and we'd also gone to Abu Dhabi to perform. In fact, while in school, I didn't do any internships, but being in music meant that throughout summers there was still a lot of work.

And being such a dedicated music student, how did you balance your time with IB?

It was hard. But you just have to make sure you know what your priorities are. There's always going to be something or the other you're going to have to compromise. I just had to make sure that music was something that was important to me. I had to put that first. And of course, I had to also put IB pretty high up there.

Were there moments when your practice time was eating into time for IB, or IB time eating into your practice sessions?

We were expected to practise eight hours a day and that was not possible for me. I definitely got in like over an hour or so. And in addition to that, I was going to music classes about four or five times a week. That's how I tried to make time for practice whenever I could.

And do you think all this hard work was also helpful towards making your application strong?

Yes, I think we need to remember that thousands of people apply from similar boards. Having something else, something strong in your application is always what will make you stand out.

And the entire application process can seem super stressful, but it's honestly not that scary. When we're applying, we're always comparing what we've done to what other people have done. I didn't do SATs/ACTs but I feel things still worked out for me because of my music. I think it's just important to focus on what you're doing rather than seeing what everybody else is doing.

Absolutely! And how were you able to highlight music, which we all know by now has been such an integral part of your life, into this one piece of application?

Through my extracurriculars, mostly. I had awards and these concerts I mentioned. In school, when there were competitions, I would win for music. In music school, we had seven-year grads. I even played for the Rocky Mountain Festival in Canada, although it was held online at the time. So I listed those down.

In the essay, too, I highlighted how it was a huge part of my life and really important to me. And I included that I was potentially looking at maybe a minor in music or working with music somehow during my time at the university. While I'm here now, I play in the UBC Symphony Orchestra. I made sure that I wrote about the possibilities of bringing my love for music and experience with it to UBC.

Thingsto Remember

↪ Spike and differentiation: Emphasize unique experiences and create a spike for your application to differentiate yourself, as Leah did with music.

↪ Focus on what you are doing, not what everybody else is doing

↪ Unfortunately, you will not be able to do everything you want to. You will have to prioritize and compromise.

University of Illinois, Urbana-Champaign: Kush Gupta

Year of graduation: 2022

Major: Computer Science and Mathematics

Other Universities Applied To: University of Washington, Seattle, Rose-Hulman Institute of Technology, University of Massachusetts, Amherst, UC Berkeley, UCLA, UC San Diego, UC Davis, UC Santa Barbara, Purdue University, Carnegie Mellon University.

High School Programme: International Baccalaureate® Diploma Programme (IBDP)

How has your college experience been so far?

I think that just being at a school which has such a high reputation for Computer Sciences has been a great experience because I am lucky to have interacted with really good faculty here. The peer group that I've created has been fantastic for me, too. It's actually been a great experience overall, trying to mix my academics with networking with people and at the same time, having fun and enjoying the college experience.

That's wonderful to know. With Computer Science as your major, what sort of career prospects or future goals are you looking at accomplishing?

My immediate goal is to get into the tech industry. I want to work at a big tech company for a while, and I'm inclined towards data science. I feel it encompasses my entire major where Mathematics and Computer Sciences come together. That's my goal for the short-term, and I'm just going to see how it goes because I want to explore how the industry really works. Based on that, I want to make my future decisions.

Have you done any internships that helped you with the decision pursue this major?

Yes, I've been interning every summer since my freshman year. I worked at Dell during three of my summers because I just liked the work environment there, and the kind of work that they're doing in data science is really cool.

I think it's pretty important to utilize the summer between each college year really well. That way you're staying updated with what you're learning and you're also applying it somewhere.

Which were the key subjects that you took in high school? Did you also have AP courses and any others that gave you extra credits and strengthened your interest?

I did my 11th and 12th in IB. So, some of my HLs were Mathematics, Computer Science and Physics, which were, of course, all important courses for me. My SLs were English, Spanish and Economics.

I actually did not take AP courses because I thought that IB itself would give me enough credits that I wanted for college. But I did do one particular course over summer - it was a development course on udemy.com in the language Swift (which is for iOS). It didn't get me any credit, but it put me into the Computer Science world pretty early on, which was really great.

And are there any particular computer languages you enjoy coding in, or any preferences?

I think my favourite one is Python. It's super easy to use and there's just so much information and libraries available for it that make it really simple. You can use it for front-end and back-end. So, Python is really my favourite, but I also enjoy C++ because it helps you understand everything in depth. C and C++ helped me build my fundamentals in Computer Science. I think these two are on the top of my list. Apart from these, I learned Java, Swift, JavaScript, quite a few of them.

Schools do offer courses in languages like Python a little bit but the syllabus is not really that comprehensive, isn't it? Did you take up any online courses, or did you teach yourself Python? I know a lot of students may want to get into coding, but they

don't know how to start learning or where to start learning.

Yes, I think the most important thing about learning how to code is understanding the fundamentals. All of these languages like C++ and Python are object-oriented languages, so if you understand the fundamentals well enough, you can really code in any language you want. The syntax is what's changing and not the fundamentals of it.

If someone really wants to start exploring CS early on, I think the best course that I've seen has been the CS50 course by Harvard University. It's a free course and it's an introduction to Computer Science. I think that will give you a good foundation.

Another thing that I would recommend is not to start off by learning CS and Python because you get too used to it being that simple. If you really want to get into the depths of computers, then maybe a good place to start would be C++ or Java.

Moving on to a big question and probably one of the questions that most students are interested in. Which extracurriculars really supported your application to universities?

I think the most important one that helped me build my profile around CS was this programme that I did at Cisco. It was essentially a six-month-long Talent Cloud programme. We worked in groups where we actually created our own projects. So in our case, we were building a college application software, which could give you all the information that you needed. It also had an essay rater, which we tried to build using machine learning. A lot of this stuff was pretty basic but I thought it gave us a good understanding of some of the fundamentals that we wanted to learn. Also, we were building something there, so talking about that experience within the application really helped me strengthen it.

Some of the other things I engaged in included some community service. I took part in a lot of sports in school and held a few leadership positions as well. I think that helped me just get a perspective to add to my essays, which eventually stood out in the application.

So, considering that you were a part of this six-month-long programme, how did you balance your time because the 10th grade has boards and the 11th and 12th have the rigorous IB programme? How did you go about managing it all effectively?

I think that's a good question. The most important thing I thought was setting my priorities and figuring out when the deadlines for certain things were. I think the biggest priority for me initially was my school exam because that always has the highest weightage on your application. Getting your school scores right and then, getting a standardised test right is key.

Planning was where I struggled personally, initially, when I joined IB. I think a lot of people do. In such a case, mapping out everything that you need to do early on can really help you prioritise your tasks and just devote the right time and the right amount of time at the right time.

And how were you tracking whether you were sticking to your priorities and deadlines? For example, people use Google Calendar or Microsoft to-do. Did you also use any sort of tool to map out your schedule?

I went a little more traditional. I used to have sticky notes on my laptop, like the physical sticky notes and they would always be on my laptop. So, anytime I would look at the keyboard, I would see them. I think that's just how I like to do it. But some of the new tools are really good, too. I do use Google Calendars a lot these days. It's really about comfort level and what grabs your attention the quickest Sometimes, your notifications might not go off, or you have to be on your phone to get those. That's why I just prefer a physical reminder. It helps me concentrate on the work better. Any of these tools are great because you might actually forget to do some of the tasks, so you need reminders.

I'm going to go back a little bit to the summer of high school again. Were there any summer schools you went to to further your skills?

No. The only thing that I did over the summer was the Cisco programme. It started at the end of my 11th grade. I had the summer to work on it. Also, I had a lot of schoolwork that I was working on, so I did not attend summer school. With some tasks already that needed to be completed before summer school, I decided to prioritise those over going to summer school.

Can you also give us a ballpark figure of how many hours of CAS you did and what you did for it?

For me, community service was about finding the right time to do the right stuff. I didn't honestly do community service for fixed hours every week. It wasn't a fixed arrangement. I'd actually started a group with my friends. A couple of us were just working towards creating new ideas and helping underprivileged children, especially in terms of education. We were trying to raise funds and we were also trying to have events where we could help people. So, we had book reading events or we had bake sales and we raised funds through those. It wasn't a very continuous kind of a thing.

Obviously, we were putting in the effort for it every week, maybe every two weeks. The time commitment really came on certain weekends where we were at a place for four to five hours and doing the work. So it's really up to you, your schedule, and your preference on what you want to do. This arrangement worked better for me because I thought the impact that we were creating was a lot more just by having things on a larger scale. But I think either way is the right way to go.

Sounds great. You also mentioned some leadership roles that you took. Could you tell us if you think that that helped in your profile-building?

Yes. I was on the student council in tenth grade in my school; I was the head of the Art Association within the school. I think that was one of the key leadership positions for me. Also, we have a school festival every year, and it's one of the biggest ones in India. I was the head of one of the departments for that fest. I think it's really about finding different problems and explaining in your application how you could solve them or solved those earlier with the help of these leadership roles. That's what you should be looking for when you're looking for leadership roles.

Interesting! Moving on, a lot of Computer Science students that I've talked to also think it's very important to win things like hackathons. I wanted to get your opinion on that as well. Do you think winning/ attending hackathons is as important, especially if Computer Science is an area you're looking to major in? Did you participate in any such hackathons?

I think it really comes down to what your interests are. I didn't do it. The only competition that I took part in which was CS-related was the Cisco competition. At the end of it, we had to present our project in front of a few other people and a few other groups. I think it's always a good thing to show interest in the subject. But you really don't have to go to these hackathons per se to be able to do that because you're still exploring what you want to do.

If you have the opportunity and you would like to explore it, I think it's great to do it. It would help you put some things on the drawing board while writing your applications. But personally, I don't think it's necessary. It's not the thing that's going to give you an edge over someone who's equivalent to you on the application.

Finally, I would love to know if you have any final tips for building the college profile.

I think my biggest tip would just be don't do things for the sake of doing them because it shows in your essays, and that is where you're actually going to be explaining what you've done. Your essays are your key, so my advice would be to do things naturally. Do things that you like. They don't really have to be really big things. You can do stuff on a smaller scale. But if you're really gaining some perspective and some knowledge out of it, I think that goes a long way than doing something, that's really big.

As far as the essay itself is concerned, I think the timing of the essay is something to keep in mind and it really depends on how fluent you are in your writing too. My advice would be to start in the summer between 11th and 12th grade. I think it's a good time to utilise and to ponder upon what you've already done because by this point you would already be in the process of doing the things that you've built your application around, right? So, I think that's a good time to start writing your essays as drafts. You can have as many as you want. Try to put what you think is important to you and how you cope with certain situations or certain problems. It's just easy to put something down on paper if you've already experienced it. Don't try to be someone you're not, you're just going to make your life harder, and going to reduce your chances of getting into whatever you want to go to.

Things to Remember

☞ Utilise the summers for internships or courses related to your interest.

☞ Do things that are important to you and mean something to you. Fabricating information on the application or participating in something just for the sake of it will not help your chances of getting into universities.

☞ Plan well and make sure to get your school scores right.

University of Arts London: Nandini Narkar

Year of graduation: 2027

Major: Critical Practices in Fashion

Other universities that were applied to: London College of Fashion, Central Saint Martins, Nottingham Trent, Kingston, and Northumbria

High School Programme: IGCSE and IBDP

First of all, congratulations. You applied to five colleges in the UK through your UCAS submissions and got into most of them. We've spoken to candidates earlier who are pursuing their studies in the UK and they had mentioned how the focus on extracurriculars in the UK universities is less when compared to the US ones. Did you have to strictly depend on your grades, then, when thinking about the applications?

The UK usually does care about super-curriculars, which are essentially extracurriculars that are exactly in relation to your major. Because I applied for a fashion major, some things like internships and online courses or even summer programmes that I'd focused on really helped. Just doing projects and photoshoots on the side were my main extracurriculars.

And because it's such an interesting major, I'm sure the readers would be curious to find out what some common jobs in the industry are or career paths that they'd be able to follow if they chose this.

For me, it's kind of like free-balling. You can really go into any kind of career that you want. I think very common ones are definitely going into marketing or working at fashion magazines. PR is also really popular. Things like that!

Great! Coming back briefly to some of the internships and summer programmes that you did. Do you have any recommendations for good summer courses or online programmes that students can benefit from?

My major is technically a communications major. I had done two internships before the 12th grade. So the summer right after the 11th grade, I did a marketing research internship at a fashion startup, and I did a marketing and social media internship at Chumbak. Those were really helpful in boosting my profile because they were with well-established and well-reputed brands. Then I did a bunch of online courses, just simple ones, like Coursera's course on fashion history and fashion in the world of design. I took another course on fashion history from Business of Fashion, a really well-reputed website. Their courses are taught by industry professionals. I ended up doing one course in fashion styling and communications from UAL itself. That also helped me get a lot of material for my portfolio.

Understood. And you did the IB programme, right?

Yeah.

If someone doing IB was thinking about a major such as this, what subjects do you recommend they should take at the higher level and standard level?

The subjects I chose were based on my liking because, for your major, you won't really need specific subjects. I took English, History and Psychology at higher level and Math, French Ab initio and Chemistry at standard level. I recommend anyone interested in an art or fashion degree to take Art in IB because IB Art is pretty interesting and vast. You get to explore a lot of different things. For a Fashion Communications portfolio especially, I'd say that it's really helpful in coming up with material and content. I wish I had taken Art or even Design Tech. It would have made the portfolio-building process easier for me.

Do you think doing these other internships and courses on the side, then, helped you stand out? Were there any other things in your application that you feel might have helped make your case?

I think that having actual work experience in the industry definitely boosted my profile. I think getting to experience whatever you want to do, in any shape or form, is super important. Apart from that, some school work like being a marketing head at several events and the magazine editor would have helped too because it showed that I had a very avid interest.

Staying focused and talking about your goals in your SOPs is something to keep in mind. I presented very well-defined goals for what I wanted to do with this degree and talked a lot about sustainability and social change that I wanted to achieve through the industry. I think that made my application a little different.

What about the fashion portfolio per se? How do you go about that?

The portfolio is definitely the most confusing part of the application, especially for a major like fashion communication. You're doing things like journalism, photography, art, marketing and everything under it. So, you don't really know what to put in your portfolio and what to omit.

Right, so how do you decide what to include in the portfolio in the first place? For an art portfolio, it might be easier I'm guessing because the very basic necessity would be to include art pieces in it. But then as you said, fashion communication can get a bit vague

when it comes to shortlisting things for your portfolio. Tell us about that.

Yes, it would be a little different for a design major and my major. For my major, I had to include a little bit of everything. I included art pieces, some of my photography, and mixed media pieces. I also had a blog, so I took my best writing pieces and graphic design pieces from there. Last year, in January, I started working on most of my big projects, but a lot of my art pieces were the ones that I had been working on since the start of my ninth grade. I had accumulated all of those. A design portfolio would definitely need more sketches and the college you apply to might ask you for any further kind of requirements (a bit more design-oriented than purely art) which can be a little different.

Apart from the portfolio, there's also the UCAS Statement of Purpose which plays a significant role.

Yes, the UCAS statement of purpose is the main thing. I started it three months before my deadline. And I worked on it every other day and kept making drafts and asking people like my family members and some close friends to look over. I also consulted people in the industry and my English teacher to get their opinion on it. What I mainly highlighted were my strengths like the kind of work I'd already done, all my super-curriculars, what made me an asset for their course, etc., because that's the only way you get to mention all of these things.

And I think it also helps to include how you can make the best out of this course and why you're a perfect candidate for it. Make sure that whatever course you're taking is true to what you want to do. I had applied for PR and communication initially and fashion communication was an alternative. They thought that I was better suited for the latter because of the way I spoke about my affiliation with social change.

Considering that you had some work experience, did you get your letter of recommendation from the places you interned at or would you suggest that getting all from the teachers would be better?

I got my LORs from two of my teachers in school, one of them has known me for a really long time. So I think the benefit of having your school teachers do it is that they can really hype you up because they've known you for a really long time. They know how you are in the school learning environment. You have that personal touch from them. I also think that if you do get help from an external person, especially the company you interned at, and if they're a really high-ranked, well-respected person, it's a really good boost to your portfolio and your profile. I feel like if you have the option, it will be good to get both bands.

You mentioned that you incorporated some of the artwork that you had begun in the ninth grade in your portfolio. That's perhaps the perfect time when we start thinking about subjects we like, those we're interested in studying further, our majors in college etc. If you could go back to your ninth-grade self at the start of high school and give yourself three pieces of advice, what would those be?

I'd probably tell her to document things more because I feel like what I'm doing has a lot to do with making really cool projects out of very sentimental things, things that we experience or witness around us. I'd probably say, hone your photography skills from a very early age.

I'd also tell her to think about projects from the very start. Don't leave it to the last minute.

You talk about photography skills being an asset for your major. Do you remember a fun project you did in school which made it to your portfolio and supported your choice of the major?

Two of my friends sew stuff together. One of them, in fact, is pursuing Fashion Design. We did a whole fashion photography shoot, where we came up with some concepts. They sewed clothes for the shoot themselves. The whole project spanned over three days, and each of those photographs had their own intricate concepts and meanings that tied everything together. It collectively represented the chaos of youth. The project had so many different components that I was able to add it to my portfolio.

That's fantastic. And how do you think you were able to integrate your major with IB? If someone's doing a Physics major, and they've taken Physics HL, they can add their IAs and extended essays, for instance, to their portfolio. Were you able to integrate the two at all?

Yes, I actually was because I did my extended essay in Psychology, and I talked about the impact of mass media on things like body image issues and health disorders. I was able to connect that with my major because social media is a big part of communication and its impact. I think you can use your EE if your likes, your personality, and your interests are reflected in the choices you make with your EE assignments as well as later.

And final question, a large part of the portfolio also asks for your writing. You spoke about your blog. Did you also participate in writing competitions? And if you win a writing competition, can you include that in your application?

Yes, I definitely think you can. I remember researching a lot for this. The New York Times had a lot of good competitions, especially for high school students, so I'd recommend students to check those ones out.

Things to Remember

☞ Supercurriculars can help you stand out, especially in applications to universities in the UK

☞ If you are in IBDP, Art and Design Tech as your subjects can speed up the portfolio-building process and make it more diverse

☞ Start thinking about projects earlier in high school.

☞ Photography, art, writing, or other multimedia projects all can be included in the portfolio for a fashion communications major. Take inspiration from your everyday life when searching for ideas.

University of Southern California: Arnav Gandhi

Year of graduation: 2027

Major: Economics

Other universities that were applied to: United States: USC, CMU, U Michigan, UIUC, UCLA, UC Berkeley, UC San Diego, UC Santa Barbara, NYU, Cornell University, UT Austin, Boston University, Emory University, Northeastern University, Wisconsin University, Madison University, Case Western University, McAllister University, Penn State, Florida Tech, and Loyola University of Chicago. Canada: Utah, Toronto and UBC.

High School Programme: Cambridge A-Levels

Diving right in, how challenging school was for you with the A levels?

My 10th grade, i.e., the GCSE, was the year of the pandemic. The exams were given to me via mocks. I did really well in my mocks because I studied for them. I ended up getting all nines and eights. Then, transitioning to A levels for me was really about sticking with three subjects. I did Math, Economics, and Business. Luckily for me, I enjoyed going to all the three classes. I enjoyed learning. That's something I noticed because in GCSE I had to work through some subjects that I didn't enjoy. But this wasn't the case in A-levels.

Right. And what level of Math did you take?

Just standard A-level Math.

You also read out a huge list of universities you applied to. How did you manage the entire process, considering that there might have been different requirements for each, with elements like supplemental essays? On top of that, there are A-level studies as well.

Everyone is of the mindset that after you get into university, you don't need to study anymore for the high school exams. But I've learned otherwise from my family members who've been in that situation. Jobs do look at your final grades. They don't care about your predicted grades. However good your predicted grades are, they're still going to ask you what your final grades were in high school. When you're looking for internships in college, they will ask you about your high school grades.

That's why I knew that I needed to keep studying. Even though I had been applying to all these universities, I still had to get the grades. I didn't want to be in a position where I'd go for a job interview or an internship, and they'd ask me about my grades. I just tried to match my predicted grades. I wanted a good internship; if I wanted that CV to be top-notch, I really had to get the grades!

And may I ask what your A-levels were looking like grade-wise?

I met my prediction. It was an A star in Business, an A in Math, and an A in Economics.

Congrats! Did you take any AP courses in high school?

Nope. Nothing.

What about standardized testing like the ACT and SAT?

I did both. To be honest, my Math is amazing. I got full in Math in both of them, but my English has always been really bad. I did not submit it because it brought both my grades down completely. Because I didn't touch 1500, I was advised not to submit it. Ultimately, you can still make a strong application with other points. So, I didn't submit any of my grades, even though I spent a lot of money on tuition and tests. But I believe it was a learning curve.

Right. Do you have any recommendations for good resources for preparations, even if it's just for Math?

Khan Academy is a big one for online classes. I also went to an institute that prepared its students well.

Approximately, how much were you studying per week leading up to the tests? How much time do you think someone should invest in it?

I left a lot of it for the last month, I'll be honest. I was not doing timed tests until two weeks before the SAT, which I do not recommend. This was during my summer vacation, i.e., August two years ago. I was prioritising my internship in the summer because I was working with Reliance, so I had a really good internship.

I wanted that casual summer term, so I would go out with my friends every night. I should have started doing timed tests earlier, like my A levels, where I did start early. A-levels were in May and June. I started studying for my A levels in January. And I would still study 20-30 hours a week. For the SAT, I crammed it within that short span of two weeks.

I mean, it's still really impressive that you ended up with an 800 in Math in the SAT and ACT.

Yeah, I didn't have to study for Math at all. I found it very easy. But it's just the English side of things which was tough. The SAT reading in particular can get boring.

That's true. I think English is like kryptonite for most people. Math is, I think, objectively easier. I also wanted to get an idea of your extracurriculars, a bird's eye view of what you were a part of that made it to the

applications. And if you could also share how much time you would spend per week if you had to estimate.

I'm a golfer and have been playing for 15 years. I've represented my school, my city, and my country. I've also played in international tournaments. One thing I stress on a lot though is that I've used my passion for golf to be a golf coach for younger students and make some kind of a difference. I started a golf community in my school.

I think that's what they liked. They don't care so much about how you do it but how well you do something. That's why my application stood out because I would see my friends, and they would write, *I'm a golfer, I'm a cricketer, I'm a footballer, etc.* They would put multiple different things but they didn't take that one thing and use it well in the application. That's the biggest thing that I did that stood out for me.

Since covid, I also became a mini content creator. I started a TikTok account where I posted real, relatable content. That blew up to 64,000 followers over the pandemic. Again, content creation was not the thing. It was important what I did with the content I created. I worked with multiple brands to spread a positive message — United Nations, for example. I didn't take any money from them. I worked for the United Nations and we raised money for countries fighting in war like Yemen, Syria, Palestine. We sent out food packages and I used my following for the better to direct people to donate to the World Food Programme. It's just about taking that one thing you do, and taking it further. Obviously, that's what my essays were about.

And when you started your content creation, were you looking at it as an activity or were you just looking at it as a hobby on the side?

It was always a hobby for me because I've always loved the camera. Then I got subscribers and I was happy. I was doing what I wanted to do. But then slowly, I realised it was not going anywhere. I switched to short-form content. I posted a few videos and one of them blew up. That's when I began taking it a little more seriously. I started posting regularly and making content. It came to a stage where I was getting recognised for it. I would go out during peak covid, and someone would ask, *Are you the guy from the TikTok video?* Initially, it was just a hobby, but then it became something bigger.

With everything else too, how much time were you investing per week?

Once in two weeks, I would go up to my room upstairs one night and just film 20 videos. Those would be my 20 videos for the next 20 days. That's why if you see my content page, a lot of them have the same t-shirt because I filmed it all on the same day. I wasn't going to sit there every day and make one video. I didn't have time for that. I would sit for five or six hours in one stretch and make everything. I would compile ideas throughout the week for this.

And what about summers in high school? You mentioned an internship. Was that during the summer?

Between the 11th and 12th, I did an internship at Reliance Industries, which was really fun, and before that, between the 10th and 11th I interned at the financial company, Ernst and Young.

Were they both finance-oriented internships?

Yes, but no at the same time. Ernst and Young was more like auditing and looking at statements. The other one involved Communications at Reliance Industries.

How were you able to actually manage and get these internships? I know that's a big point of contention for high school students. Was it just through connections or was there any platform you used?

I'll be very honest. It's hard to get an internship if you don't have some sort of connection. Don't get me wrong, you can definitely sign up for internships, but for a big company like this, it was through connections.

What role do you think these internships actually played in your application?

They boosted it for sure. When I applied to Berkeley, I applied for Economics; when I applied to Cornell, I applied to their business school. In both these cases,

I stressed my Ernst and Young internship. Each application was different.

When I applied to Boston University, it was a marketing degree, so I could put my Reliance one in there. If I was applying for both, I just put both in. Every essay I wrote was different for the school that I wanted to apply to. Then I would push what I needed to. Does that make sense?

Right, yes. So, going back a bit to your experience with the food drive, was there any other social work that you highlighted?

There's an Operation Smile, which is in UAE. It's for kids who are born with a cleft on their smile. Millions of kids are born with a cleft palate on their lips. It lowers their ability to breathe. Operation Smile works for that surgery. I did a fundraiser with them and worked with them for a while.

Apart from that, I worked with my aunt in Mumbai. I also worked with animal shelters in the South as well. A couple of summers ago, I worked with them. I mentioned that. There were a couple of small things, but they sent a letter saying thank you for your efforts which helped.

With respect to the food drive, how do you actually manage to get in contact with the UN and actually start working with them?

They contacted me actually.

Okay, so they saw that you had a platform on social media and then reached out to you.

Right.

What about awards, prizes, competitions, Olympiads? Did you mention those?

I've been playing golf for 15 or so years. I've got like 40 trophies in golf. I won the UAE junior championship before. I mentioned all of that. I was in my school cricket team. Even though I didn't stress on that that much, I did still put that in my award section. I won the cricketer of the year twice in my school. Apart from that, I played the guitar. I won lots of competitions. I just put in every single thing I possibly had, the ones I thought were big. If it was like a small swimming medal that I got in second grade or a running athletic medal, I wouldn't put that in. But anything significant, I added to the awards.

We did speak about your internships during the summers. Were those the kind of things you focused on throughout the summer break?

I had so much fun during my summers. I've managed my life well I'd like to believe. For my 11th grade summer, I did my Reliance internship during the day, that was from 10 am to 6 pm.

Then in the evenings, I'd go to the gym or just relax. That happened for a couple of weeks. For the next couple of weeks, I did SAT tuitions from 12 noon to 4 pm every day. Then at least in the afternoon, I could go out with my friends and play badminton. I did this on the weekdays. On weekends, I could still go out in the night.

Finally, then, what was the overall application process like for you? You did apply to Canada and UK as well, apart from the US. Was your school enough to help you with the entire bit?

I did have a counsellor, yes. I had a counsellor based in Dubai; she was amazing.

Do you recommend getting a counsellor?

You don't have to, but if you don't know what you want to do, I think they're a good guiding point. But you have to go by reviews; talk to people, ask. My recommendation for anyone who wants to look for a counsellor, especially Indian counsellors who are really very expensive, do extensive research first, ask for reviews, and then make a choice.

What led you to pick the US over both Canada and the UK?

To be honest, the US had always been my dream. I got a full ride scholarship with two of the universities in Canada, including UBC. It was surprising because they barely give full ride to international students. I chose USC with no scholarship just for the fact that it's been my dream school.

And what about the UK? Since you did the GCSE A-level system, wouldn't it have been easier to transition to the UK?

It would have. Taking that path would have been much easier. Even the application process for the UK universities is nothing compared to the US process. I did my entire UK application over one weekend. But I've always wanted the college experience in the US.

Great. What about letters of recommendation? How many did you submit?

I submitted to one from my counsellor at school and one from my Math teacher who liked me.

How did you go about picking the teacher?

That one teacher you know that will only boost your ego and who genuinely likes you will write a genuinely good letter of recommendation.

As far as the essays are concerned, how did you approach them when you started writing them?

I made an outline. I would write down small subheadings below every point. Then I'd write the essay.

Something like the Common App which is kind of like a show more than a tell kind of an essay, right? How do you go about idea generation for that and honing in on the right Common App essay from a host of prompts and ideas?

I chose mine because I knew what I wanted to write my story about. Just think about what you can get the most out of. Not the fact that it's the easiest to write. My problem was not the easiest to write for sure.

But then just whatever you have the most information about, that you know you can write the most about, do that.

What about supplemental essays? How do you go about tackling all of them?

I could use some information even though most of it was new. I would always have an outline. I would never write baselessly ever. Make an outline and maybe just jot some ideas down there; that will help.

If you had to go back to your high school self, and if there were other kids in your position, what final advice would you give them?

This people say all the time but it's so true. It's the quality, not the quantity. Essentially, it's what you do, not how much you do.

Three Things to Remember

☞ Try to apply your passion to multiple aspects of your life (social service, honours and awards, etc.). By doing this you demonstrate sustained interest and commitment.

☞ Emphasize different parts of your application for different schools/programs that you are applying to. Not every application to every school has to be the same, even though you are the same person who has done the same activities, etc.

☞ Your predicted grades are not everything. Even after you get admission to universities with predicted grades, your final grades matter for future internships and job applications.

SOME HELPFUL RESOURCES

A List of Online Courses to Check Out & Boost Your Profile

STEM

- Harvard University's CS50 course (on Edx)
- University of Michigan's Mindware: Critical Thinking for the Information Age (on Coursera)
- University of Arizona's Astronomy: Exploring Time and Space (on Coursera)
- Yale University's Financial Markets (on Coursera)
- University of Pennsylvania's Introductory Series to Finance and Accounting (on Coursera)
- Harvard University's Science & Cooking: From Haute Cuisine to Soft Matter Science (on Edx)
- Stanford University's course on Game Theory (on Coursera)

ARTS & HUMANITIES

- Harvard University's Masterpieces of World Literature (on Edx)
- Harvard University's Shakespeare's Life and Work (on Edx)

- ✎ Introduction to Philosophy by University of Edinburgh (on Coursera)

- ✎ MoMA's (The Museum of Modern Art) Fashion as Design (on Coursera)

- ✎ Business of Fashion's Fashion History for Today (on Business of Fashion)

A Guide to Writing the Common App Essay

The essay section has the potential to be the most unique part of your application. It gives you 650 words which enable you to communicate **who you are** and **why you would be successful at that college.** Even though these are some of the most important criteria an admissions officer considers, it is almost impossible to elaborate upon these aspects in any other part of your application. Nevertheless, a strong essay will help you do so and make your application stand out from the other thousand applications that an admissions officer has to read. Here are some things that will help you sail through the essay.

WHAT?

- This is a platform to show the admissions officer a part of your personality that isn't reflected in other elements of your application. These are essays that are grounded in personal experiences (preferably during high school).

- Jay Rameshwar advises us:

    - Find **what makes you unique** and focus on that in the essays to stand out.

↯   At the same time, Harshita Singh also warns us:

  ↯   Don't be in the pursuit of having a unique essay per se. You don't want to fabricate a version of yourself. There's a difference between having a unique *essay* and writing about what makes *you* different and interesting. **Be true to yourself.** Your essay must sound authentic.

HOW?

↯   According to a report documented in the Wall Street Journal, admissions officers in most top colleges spend approximately 8 minutes or less per essay. This means that you need to get two things right in your essays –

  ↯   Great essays have great structures. You want to help them by using a structure that helps them with clarity on what you want to do, why you want to do it, what makes you a great candidate, etc. They don't want to spend extra minutes navigating their way through a badly organised essay trying to find what exactly you're interested in.

  ↯   Knowing exactly *who* your audience is makes it easier for you to shortlist and write the right thing for the right university. Include parts of you that you think are relevant to the department at the university you're applying to.

  ↯   Mehak Kapoor shares some points that further these:

☞ Make sure that you have an outline of each paragraph. Each paragraph should have an idea because you have to make the essay interesting. The top and the bottom of the essay can be inspirational. Try to link the paragraphs to each other, if possible.

☞ You don't want to write: *I'm good at this. I'm good at this. And I'm good at this.* Build a storyline, and write your story.

☞ While Arnav Gandhi supports the idea of streamlining information for different applications. In his opinion, you can put specific parts of your extracurriculars and leave out some depending on what course and university you're applying to. For instance, if you're applying for a marketing programme, you can focus on your internships in marketing, communications etc. If you're applying for a theatre degree in a different institute, you shouldn't write the same application you've written for the marketing course. Be smart about this.

WHEN TO START?

☞ A good student begins thinking about their essay a year before submitting it. You don't want to overthink but you also don't want to delay it too much. There is no one time that is the right time. Essays can be written and built over weeks or months.

☞ One of the benefits of starting early is that you get to have it reviewed as well. You could request 2 or 3 people you trust to guide you and share their honest feedback.

☞ Kush Gupta advises us:

   ☞ To use the summer before the 12th grade to get started on your essay, and **write as many drafts as you want.**

☞ For Vihaan Shah, getting done with at least one good draft at this time is important:

   ☞ The only essay that you can realistically write before the 12th grade starts is your Common App essay. Get that done, get it out of the way because you have the time. You don't have school, and colleges release their essays after school starts.

☞ Sarvesh Rajkumar agrees and tells us that his best essay ideas came this way in his shower. Look at essay prompts early and start thinking about ideas. By being in that frame of mind, he was able to brainstorm without the pressure of studies and other school work.

SUPPLEMENTAL ESSAY

Some colleges ask you to write a supplemental essay. These are additional essays (along with the Common App Essay) which are shorter than the Common App and often help the admissions officers have a more concrete idea of how you would fit in. Common supplemental essays include, "Why this college", "Why this major", etc. These are a great way to help you stand out and demonstrate your interest in a college.

Two Quick Pieces of Advice

- Ronit's golden rule is:

- If you can just copy and paste a *Why X School?* essay into another application and just change the name and say *Why Z School?* then the essay is not strong enough. **If it can just be taken as a template and moved around, it's too generic.**

- Naaz leaves us with a great way to execute this advice:

- Make an Excel sheet or open a simple Word document. **Write down important details of the universities you plan to apply to.** For example, the professors in your major, certain locations (facilities on campus, extracurriculars they offer, the classes you would probably be interested in). This will make it easier to write about specific elements that attract you to the university.

- Make sure you have researched well!

MY CHECKLIST

As you step into high school, take a moment to set your goals for the year!

I am: ____

I study in: ____

My dream major is: ___________________________________

My dream university/college is: _________________________

____

Colleges I'd like to apply to: __________________________

____

____

____

My subjects in high school are/will be: _________________

____

____

____

I'm good at or want to be good at: _____________________

____

____

____

Workshops/courses I'd like to attend: _________________

____

____

____

Competitions/exams I'd like to attend: _______________

____

____

____

Community service I have/will be doing:

____

____

____

____

Extra-curriculars (internships, research papers, leadership roles, etc.) I have taken part/will take part in:

____

____

____

____